Women Seeking Intimacy with God

Fifty-Two Devotionals of Wisdom and Truth from Women of the Bible

Helen Holmes

ISBN 979-8-89043-872-0 (paperback)
ISBN 979-8-89043-873-7 (digital)

Christian Faith Publishing
832 Park Avenue
Meadville, PA 16335
www.christianfaithpublishing.com

Printed in the United States of America

This book is dedicated to a couple of people who impacted my life in a powerful way. The first one is my second born son who departed this life in October, 2018. His name is Gregory (Greg) Stuart Neasley. Greg was the baby of the family for nine years, then came a sister and another brother. As far as Greg was concerned he was always the baby. He didn't say this but it was his expectation. God warned me a month before Greg's sudden death due to an aneurysm or stroke. I did not understand what the warning was about but it prepared me for his departure. I went through the stages of grief. But at the "feeling of guilt" stage, God said to me, "the best thing that you could have done for your children was to bring them to me." Greg accepted Christ at the age of nine. I gave birth to four children and I'm grateful to God, they all have accepted Christ.

A smile comes across my face when I think of my big sister, Min. Johnnie Mae Johnson. She was my only sister. She departed this life in January, 2022. She was my BFF, my confidant and my fellow laborer in ministry. We supported and encouraged each other in the ups and downs of life. Always reminding each other of what the Word says in light of our situation.

I miss these two individuals and look forward to our reunion in heaven.

Foreword

When Helen contacted me to ask me to write a foreword for her upcoming book that is based on the Christian blogs she has written, I was happy to put into words how much I appreciated and anticipated her weekly writings. I knew that Helen is a godly woman before I ever met her. I worked with her husband for several years and gleaned from conversations we had about our families that she is a compassionate, intelligent woman who puts Christ first in her decision-making. When I had the good fortune to meet her, my view of her was confirmed. And when I learned that she was writing weekly blogs called *Women Seeking Intimacy with God*, I wanted to be on her mailing list. Each Monday, I opened my emails and looked for her wisdom for the week. Her writings were uplifting and encouraging and applicable for the journey through this life that we all find ourselves upon. My eyes were opened as she wrote about the women in the Bible who experienced some of the same trials and tribulations that we women face today. Through it all, God's grace shone through the lives of those women and encouraged me with whatever situation I found myself at the time. Sometimes, it was simply a blog of praise and reminded me of the many blessings that we enjoy and are able to share with others.

I am looking forward with much anticipation to being able to find Helen's blogs in book form and keep it handy for instant lessons from this godly and loving woman.

Joy Hart

I can say, without a doubt, that this book of devotions helped me through some of the toughest seasons of my life. Every devotional I read aligned with where I was spiritually, mentally, and emotionally. It felt as though the author was writing directly to me. I am so honored to have tasted the goodness of *Women Seeking Intimacy with God*, and I know you will be touched by it too.

Ashanti Watson

Introduction

I was called into the ministry in 1995. I taught in my local church and accepted speaking engagements in other local churches, nonprofits and once at a baccalaureate event.

In 2007, during my quiet time with the Lord, the faces of five local women with whom I had attended church about 30 years previous to that time. I heard these words, "I want you to do for the single moms what those ladies did for you while you were a single mom. I was a single mom in between marriages. I attended church with these older ladies who loved me and my two little boys. Plus, they exemplified the lifestyle of devout Christian ladies. They each played a different role in my life. What they all had in common was the way they loved me and my boys.

In that year I founded (SMILE) Single Moms Inspired to Live with Excellence. The Lord gave me the acronym S.M.I.L.E. and told me to teach them from the book of Ephesians. My goal was to teach them who they were in Christ and guide them to develop a personal intimate relationship with him.

All of my ministry efforts since then is to encourage women to come close to God, and God will come close to you. (James 4:8a NLT)

I began blogging in 2019. I entitled it "Women Seeking Intimacy with God." In 2021, I was led to blog about the women of the Bible. After writing and posting on my website and social media, I felt the unction to publish a book using the blogs I had written in 2021.

What you are about to read is the result of much prayer, study, meditating, and writing what I believe God had inspired me to write.

The women of the Bible have a lot to say to us today. They impacted the nation of Israel but also the world and beyond. Their uniqueness helped to shape the Bible story. They will continue to be remembered for centuries to come.

My purpose in writing a series on women of the Bible is not to retell their story. I suggest you read the Bible to get their full story. Hopefully, this will inspire you to search out their story. As I embarked on this journey, my focus was on one or two things we could learn from these ladies.

This is a side issue. Remember when Jesus fed the 5,000 or the 4,000. He gathered up the fragments. He threw nothing away. That's the way he handles our lives, the good, the bad and the ugly. In scripture, He told the whole story. So, we can learn from the good things they did as well as the bad. Actually, that applies to our lives too.

Let nothing be wasted in your life. Learn and grow from the good and the bad things that happen in your life. Don't waste your time being ashamed of the things that happened in your life or being condemned. Use it to grow. God loves and accepts you regardless. You're His daughter, the apple of his eye. I can hear Jesus tell the woman caught in adultery, "neither do I condemn thee, go and sin no more." Read John 8:11b.

It gave me abundant joy looking deep into the lives of these ladies. I was able to see in the Old Testament how God orchestrated the events of their lives. As I looked, I could see how everything was preparing the way for Jesus to come to the earth. In the New Testament, he used the women to help build and advance the gospel of the kingdom.

Day 1

Lady Eve

And God said, Let us make man in our image, after our likeness: and let them have dominion over the fish of the sea, and over the fowl of the air, and over the cattle, and over all the earth, and over every creeping thing that creepeth upon the earth. So God created man in his own image, in the image of God created he him; male and female created he them.

—Genesis 1:26–27

Adam was the first man that God created. Eve was the first woman God made to be a companion and helper to Adam. I see God acting as Eve's father when He gives her hand in marriage to the groom, Adam. There was no preacher to say, "Who gives this woman…" but I can imagine God's heart was beaming as He presented His masterpiece to Adam.

What can we learn from Lady Eve? One thing that I had to come to terms with is that Eve was first influenced by her lustful desires. In other words, she succumbed to the temptations of Satan because she was eyeing the tree of the knowledge of good and evil. Satan, in all his subtlety, seized the opportunity to mislead her. Read Genesis chapter 3.

What can we learn? Number 1, don't have a conversation with the devil. Don't try to reason with what you know is wrong. Don't try to justify what the Word clearly says is sin. Number 2, if you know you have a weakness in certain areas, separate yourself from it or him. Eve was already at the tree. Why, Eve? You know what God said!

A high school teacher once told me, "If you play with fire, you'll get burned. If you play with trash, you'll get it in your eye. If you lay down with a dog, you'll get up with fleas." I was entertaining a young man that I knew was too experienced for me. I needed that warning. He went on to get another girl pregnant.

Temptation is not a sin. Yielding is the sin. Jesus was tempted by the same devil with the same temptations with which Eve was tempted. These are the same temptations he tries on us today (1 John 2:16). He doesn't have any new tricks. Jesus didn't try to reason with the devil. He simply replied with "it is written," then said, "Get thee behind me, Satan" (Matthew 4:1–10).

Another thing I kept trying to see is how Eve influenced Adam to eat of the tree of the knowledge of good and evil when he was by her side when Eve and Satan had this conversation. He heard the whole conversation. How did he allow himself to be influenced when he received the command straight from God Himself? Was it his selfish desires also? She didn't manipulate or trick him. But sometimes, just because someone whom you love does a thing, you rationalize within yourself, *It must be okay. After all, she didn't fall down dead when she ate it.*

Maybe God didn't really mean it. Maybe He changed His mind. Not so! Not so!

So what can we learn from this? Eve influenced Adam to do evil. Have you ever influenced anyone to do evil? What does the Word say about being an influencer? We all have the capability to influence others to do evil or to do good. There are consequences for influencing others to do evil.

All of mankind fell the day that Adam was influenced to do evil. There are consequences when we cause others to do evil. Read Matthew 18:5–6. The Word tells us how to avoid being influenced by evil. Read Proverbs 7:1–5. Also, Romans 12:1–2 instructs us on how to not be influenced by the world. We are all influencers in one way or another. Jesus tells us to be influencers for good. When we follow Him, that's our greatest assignment. He equips us so we will be good influencers. Read Matthew 5:13–16 and Acts 1:8.

Paul told Timothy that he knew his grandmother Lois and mother Eunice were great influencers in his life. Read 2 Timothy 1:5. If you're an influencer for good, your legacy may last for generations to come, even centuries.

Paul was a great influencer. He encouraged the early Christians to mimic the things they learned, received, heard, and saw him do. Read Philippians 4:9. Thousands of years later, we're still endeavoring to do that. Abel is yet influencing today because of his faith. Read Hebrews 11:4.

Think about the ones who personally influenced you to do good. Ask God to help you be a good influencer.

Day 2

Lady Sarai or Sarah

*And Abram and Nahor took them wives: the name of Abram's
wife was Sarai; and the name of Nahor's wife, Milcah, the
daughter of Haran, the father of Milcah, and the father
of Iscah. But Sarai was barren; she had no child.*
—Genesis 11:29–30

God chose Sarai to be Abram's wife and ultimately to be "mother of nations." God knew that Sarai would be a devoted wife to Abram. Sarai was a beautiful woman inside and out. Sarai was a holy and godly woman who followed her husband's leadership. Her beauty came from within from a gentle and peaceful spirit. She had the makings of a "princess."

I found no record of her nagging and complaining about them living a nomadic lifestyle, roaming about from place to place. She supported her husband when he told her God said, "Leave your country and kinsmen and go to a place I will show you."

That might have played out differently today when many of us wives might have said, "Now look here, Abram. You want me to leave the comfort of my home and follow you to only God knows where? Are you sure you heard right? I've never heard of a god telling a person to go somewhere without telling them where to go. And besides that, you said He said you will have as many descendants as the stars in the sky and the sand on the seashore. Where are you supposed to get them? I'm barren and sixty-five years old."

I heard none of this from Sarai, whose name was later changed to Sarah. The Word tells us as wives, we're to be like the holy women of old; and Sarah, "our mother," is our example. Read 1 Peter 3:1–6 (TPT).

As I examined these scriptures, Sarah never used words that were put-downs or sarcastic to her husband. The Word says, "A gentle and quiet or peaceful spirit is precious to God." That's the kind of wife Sarah was. Plus, she called him master or lord. Now that's not a term that we would use today. But maybe it's the equivalent of us calling him words of endearment like *honey, sweetie, baby, sugar, dear, sweetheart*, etc.

Another scripture to support what God is pleased with is found in Proverbs 25:15 (KJV), "By long forbearing is a prince persuaded, and a soft tongue breaketh the bone." This same verse in The Passion Translation (TPT) says, "Use patience and kindness when you want to persuade leaders and watch them change their minds right in front of you. For your gentle wisdom will quell the strongest resistance." Your husband is the prince and leader of your household. Does this scripture speak to you on how to respond to him? I must admit it speaks to me loud and clear.

Another scripture you're probably familiar with is also Proverbs 15:1 (KJV), "Soft answer turneth away wrath: but grievous words stir up anger." The TPT says, "Respond gently when you are confronted and you'll defuse the rage of another. Responding with sharp, cutting words will only make it worse. Don't you know that being angry can ruin the testimony of even the wisest of men?"

This sounds so good. I do want to emulate Sarah. However, Sarah did have her moments of outburst when dealing with Hagar and her son. But I must confess I have a ways to go. I don't put my husband down, but if he snaps at me, then (sometimes) I snap back. We don't get out of hand because one of us will hush. Usually it's him. But I want him to understand what I'm saying or how I feel.

This is definitely an area I need to continue to work on. I have been working on this and am somewhat better. I know I'm not the only one who can use some improvement in this area, right?

I'm taking these verses, reading, and meditating on them. This is one way the truth will make you free. Read John 8:32.

Sarah waited a very long time to give birth—even past childbearing age. She became impatient and did the unthinkable. She gave her handmaiden to be wife to her husband and bear him a child. She was a desperate woman. What can we learn from this decision?

We dare not judge or condemn her. Sarah was about seventy-five, and her situation was looking hopeless. To add insult to injury, the Lord had reaffirmed His covenant with Abram (chapter 15). So maybe she wanted to help God accomplish His promise. Also, did I mention that it was a shame for women to not bear children?

Sometimes, waiting becomes a challenge. Waiting is a virtue that needs development. The Word says in Psalm 27:14, one of my favorites to meditate on in the TPT,

> Here's what I've learned through it all: Don't give up; don't be impatient; be entwined as one with the Lord. Be brave and courageous, and never lose hope. Yes, keep on waiting—for he will never disappoint you!

Now, of course, Sarah didn't have the scriptures to hold on to. She knew of the Lord, but Abraham is the one who had a relationship with Him, although she may have worshipped every time Abraham built an altar to the Lord. To trust in, hope for, and expect a thing to happen, you must become entangled and intertwined with the Lord. You can't say "I'm waiting on the Lord" and not seek His face or seek His Word on the subject like "wait." Plus, you must meditate on the Word so you can get it deep in your heart and soul. That's how you gain strength and courage to wait and not give up or lose heart.

There are other verses on waiting on the Lord like Psalm 62:5 and 37:34 and Isaiah 40:31, to name a few. When you look at Genesis chapters 15 and 16, you'll see that both Abram and Sarai had a moment of questioning or doubt. Oh, but God came to their rescue and changed Abram's name to Abraham, "father of nations." Then He changed Sarai's name to Sarah, "mother of nations." So now when they hear their name called or when they introduce themselves, they hear "father of nations" and "mother of nations."

Confessing a thing in faith that lines up with the Word helps it to manifest. Sarah went on to produce a man-child that God named Isaac. She was ninety, while Abraham was one hundred years old. God kept His promise even though it was a long time coming. Don't give up on what God has promised you.

Day 3

Lady Hagar

The angel of the LORD said to her, "Return to your mistress, and submit to her authority."
— Genesis 16:9

Thereafter, Hagar used another name to refer to the LORD, who had spoken to her. She said, "You are the God who sees me." She also said, "Have I truly seen the One who sees me?"
—Genesis 16:13

Read Genesis 16:6–16.

It's difficult to look at this story and not judge it through the eyes of our Western culture and in today's time. Although it seemed harsh the way Sarah and Abraham treated Hagar, it was not uncommon and looked upon as the thing to do. However, the hurt Hagar experienced is no different from what a woman would feel today if she received such unfair treatment.

So this article will only deal with Hagar's perspective and not the wrongness or rightness of Sarah and Abraham's actions.

There are two incidents where Hagar leaves the camp of Abraham and Sarah. The first time, she runs away. The second time, she is sent away with her son (Genesis 21:10–21). Each time, God finds her and ministers to her. Why did He do that? Why did He take such interest in Hagar? God loves everyone. It doesn't matter your status in life or the color of your skin. He loves us all equally. In looking at the big picture, God had a plan that would lead to the salvation of all mankind, at least to those who receive it. He chose Abram and his descendent by which this salvation would come to all mankind. Too bad so many will not receive this gift of love from a loving God.

We see in the passage cited above that Hagar runs away after she has become pregnant and is now treated harshly by her mistress, Sarai. Of course, there is understandably contention between these two women. So Hagar thought it necessary to leave the camp. The problem is that this is a wilderness area and she is all alone, a slave, and pregnant. She sat by a spring of water, pondering her situation. Who could help her? It all seemed so hopeless.

We all love those moments when we look back and say, "But God…" Hagar had no provisions to take care of herself and her unborn child, but God sent His angel to find her. We often sing the song "He's an On-Time God."

We as born-again children of God must realize there is no hopeless situation when we put our trust in God. We may not be able to see a way out. But if we stand on the Word that prescribes what we need to do, like in Proverbs 3:5–7, then everything will work out for your good and His glory. The prescription from the Message Bible makes it very plain what we must do.

> Trust GOD from the bottom of your heart;
> don't try to figure out everything on your own.
> Listen for GOD's voice in everything you do, everywhere you go; he's the one who will keep you on track.
> Don't assume that you know it all.
> Run to GOD! Run from evil! (Proverbs 3:5–7 MSG)

Now you can't beat the prescription. The trouble is that a lot of Christians don't take the time to follow it. They want to do it their way.

What if Hagar had not followed the angel's instructions when he told her to go back and submit to her mistress. She and her unborn baby probably would have died. I think many times we fail to win the battle because we fail to do what the Word tells us to do.

Day 4

Lady Rebekah

*And she said, Drink, my lord: and she hasted, and let down
her pitcher upon her hand, and gave him drink. And when
she had done giving him drink, she said, I will draw water
for thy camels also, until they have done drinking. And she
hasted, and emptied her pitcher into the trough, and ran again
unto the well to draw water, and drew for all his camels.*
— Genesis 24:18–20

The story of Rebekah is found mainly in chapters 24 to 28 of Genesis. Remember what I said in the beginning of this journey: God tells and uses the good, the bad, and the ugly. Again, we'll see two sides of this lady. This should help us not to be such critics when we see Christians exhibit two sides. I know we have an edge because we're born-again and have the Holy Spirit.

However, we still have a free will and the influence of the old nature (the flesh). I just want us to give people more grace, which is what God gives us.

This story opens up with Abraham giving his servant instructions to go find Isaac a wife among his kinsmen. He didn't want Isaac marrying a Canaanite woman. The servant met up with Rebekah as he finished praying for help. She was coming to draw water from the well.

He prayed a specific prayer that would let him know the woman the Lord had chosen. Everything worked out as he had prayed. Rebekah presented herself to be a very hospitable woman. When he asked her for a drink of water, she said, "Sure, and I'll also draw some for your camels" (paraphrased).

He had ten camels and men who drove them. She provided water for the whole company of men and camels. I believe she did it with a smile and not grudgingly. I hope the men assisted her. This is an excellent example of the spirit of hospitality. There are people who have the gift of hospitality (Romans 12:13). But all of God's people should be hospitable people. However, that's not always the case.

Have you seen Christians who always have a scowl look on their face? Or have you been to someone's home or church and you didn't really feel welcome, even though on the church program there is a welcome address? There is an atmosphere of uptight, tense, and unfriendliness. I looked up the word *hospitable* to fully understand what it means. *Webster's Dictionary* says, "Generous and friendly treatment of visitors and guests; the activity of providing food, drinks, etc. for people who are the guests or customers of an organization; generous and friendly to guests or visitors; offering a pleasant or sustaining environment."

Hebrews 13:2 (NLT) says, "Don't forget to show hospitality to strangers, for some who have done this have entertained angels without realizing it!" There are people who work in positions and should be hospitable, but they are not.

I've driven up to the fast-food window to receive my food, and the attendant barely looks at me and certainly doesn't have a smile. I've wondered about their training. There is one fast-food chain where the workers are always serving with a smile. When you say thank you, they say with a smile, "My pleasure." I'll bet you know which one I'm talking about. I love friendly service. Then there are positions at church where people should be hospitable. One of my sons attended a church where he served on the parking lot team. His pastor said he was friendly and always served with a smile. He had an infectious smile. When I visited there, the parking lot team and greeters all the way to our seat welcomed us there with a smile. If we each did a self-examination, on a scale of 1 to 10, where would we rank in hospitality? If we're honest, there is probably room to grow. In these times in which we live, there are so many needs that could use a good dose of generosity. When you see a neighbor or sister or brother in Christ who lack the bare necessities, what do you do? When people come to your church, do you go out of your way to be friendly and make them feel welcomed? Yes, you may have a hospitality committee, but you don't have to be on a committee to show hospitality. Rebekah's story gets a little long and complicated years later. We will continue this story in the next blog.

Day 5

Lady Rebekah Part 2

*Isaac loved Esau because he enjoyed eating the wild game
Esau brought home, but Rebekah loved Jacob.*
—Genesis 25:28

*At the age of forty, Esau married two Hittite wives: Judith, the
daughter of Beeri, and Basemath, the daughter of Elon. But
Esau's wives made life miserable for Isaac and Rebekah.*
—Genesis 26:34–35

Now let's observe Rebekah several years later after she has given birth to twins. She was barren at first, like Sarah, but Isaac prayed for her (Genesis 25:21). She conceived twins. While carrying the children in her womb, they were so active that Rebekah prayed about it. God revealed that there were two nations inside of her, and the older would serve the younger. So then as the boys grew, they had some relationship issues that may have been fueled by the fact that Isaac loved Esau best and Rebekah loved Jacob best.

This was a very dysfunctional family, as many of our families can be nowadays. There was a lot of manipulation and deception going on, as well as favoritism. When raising children, it's important that they see our integrity. Integrity (the quality of being honest and fair) should be one of your character traits as a Christian. That's just who you are, or it should be.

You know the story of Job, who lost all his possessions, including his ten children. Then Satan attacked his health. Then his wife asked him, "Dost thou still retain thine integrity? curse God, and die" (Job 2:9). When all that happened to Job, he remained an honest, fair, and upright man. People get themselves in so much trouble today by trying to circumvent the law by trying to be clever and just dishonest.

What does Proverbs 22:1 tell us? "A good name is rather to be chosen than great riches, and loving favor rather than silver and gold." If you're dishonest, it mars your reputation, your good name. If you want your children to grow up and be honest, abiding citizens, they must first observe it in you. Proverbs 20:7 (NLT) says "The just man walketh in his integrity: his children are blessed after him."

Parents are the child's first teachers. Children are going to imitate their parents or guardians before they imitate anyone else. Rebekah also exhibited traits of deception and manipulation. No doubt Jacob observed this all his life. Rebekah thought she was doing a good thing because God had told her, before the twins were born, that the older one would serve the younger one.

So she went about to cause Jacob to receive the firstborn blessings. She had a well-crafted plan to trick or deceive her husband. Read Genesis 27:5–17.

Rebekah was very determined and had no remorse. This probably wasn't her first time doing things like this. She wants to make sure things turn out the way God told her. Have we really learned in today's time we don't have to try to help God out? God is God all by Himself. He did not need Rebekah's help. If God tells you He's going to do a certain thing through you or He has called you for a specific purpose, you do not need to bogart your way. Keep it in prayer, ask for clarity, study, wait on God, and listen for the leading of the Holy Spirit. God has a way and His sovereign timing.

Look at what these parents are doing to their children by their deception and manipulation. You know Esau is reacting to family dynamics by going and marrying not one but two Hittite women who caused his dad and mom to be miserable (Genesis 26:35). I don't know if this was God's plan the way things turned out. But God has a way of using everything we present to Him. But I believe life would have been easier if things had been left to God.

This also blessed me. Even though Jacob may have learned to be a trickster or supplanter from his mom, God got him ready to be used by Him when Jacob encountered the angel of the Lord and wrestled with him (Genesis 32:24–28). In this encounter, the Lord changed his name from Jacob, "supplanter or con man," to Israel, meaning "prince of God." His name and his character were changed.

The reason this part blessed me is that after being raised in a dysfunctional family that taught him to be a "con man," God changed him. God had a purpose for his life. Regardless of how we are raised, God can change us or our children. He has a purpose for you and me. I thank God He changed me.

Day 6

Lady Leah

*And Laban had two daughters: the name of the elder was
Leah, and the name of the younger was Rachel.*
—Genesis 29:16

*And it came to pass, that in the morning, behold, it was Leah: and
he said to Laban, What is this thou hast done unto me? did not I
serve with thee for Rachel? wherefore then hast thou beguiled me?*
—Genesis 29:25

In my previous studies and as being taught, I've not given much thought to Leah. It was always Rachel because that is who Jacob worked so hard to get. I guess I'm a romantic. My focus has been on how Jacob was being deceived (you reap what you sow) and the satisfaction that he finally got the woman he so loved and desired. But Leah was described as having weak eyes and no sparkle. Another translation said she had soft eyes, but Rachel was stunningly beautiful (Genesis 29:17).

The bulk of this story is found in Genesis 29:15, 30:24. Both sisters are mentioned in later chapters. But this set of scriptures speak more about their relationship with each other. When I was studying these passages, the word *rejection* floated across my mind. I decided not to get caught up in the fact that Jacob practiced polygamy. That was a cultural thing in that day. Both of these sisters had to follow the customs of the day, whether they liked it or not.

Leah said at one point, "You stole my husband." Rachel was jealous that Leah was having babies and she was not. Leah felt rejected throughout her marriage. God took notice of this treatment. He was gracious and blessed her to have six boys and a girl, also two more boys by her handmaiden.

Before this study, I did not notice that God not only blessed her in her present situation, but He chose her to be the mother of Judah, who is the tribe of the lineage of Jesus. What a high honor God has bestowed upon her. Leah could not have known that God had chosen her to bless the whole world. What does this say for us? When we are going through rough times as a child of God, keep your focus on Him; trust Him; and walk an obedient, upright life. How you live and what you do will affect generations to come. God has a purpose and a plan. God sees the end from the beginning (Isaiah 46:10).

Now let's look at the word *rejection*. Other words associated with rejection are *not accepted, not preferred*, and *not good enough*. I know men and women have received rejection. There is a song that says, "When you can't be with the one you love, love the one you're with." To a woman, that's a form of rejection. It says in essence, "I can't be with the one I really love, so I'll just be with you." I heard a young woman say she got pregnant by a man. Of course, she thought he was going to marry her. When she was three months pregnant, he married someone else. She felt rejected. Eventually, she picked up the pieces of her life and is now serving God in a powerful way. Recently, she got married.

Maybe you've felt rejected as a child. One sibling was preferred over another. Maybe you felt rejected because you were too skinny; too fat; skin tone too dark; skin tone too light; hair too short, kinky, not silky enough. You had freckles and wore thick glasses. Maybe you felt rejected because your father was not active in your life. You feel like your birth was accidental. Maybe you were a victim of sexual abuse, and now you feel you're not good enough. Maybe you were not accepted by your peers, bullied, poked fun at, or rejected by coworkers or the religious community.

Rejection can leave a deep wound and scar that warps your personality. It can cause all kinds of social behaviors to erupt. I have some good news. If you've been rejected, count it all as joy. You're in good company. Jesus suffered rejection by his family, community (Luke 4:24), and religious leaders. He understands how you feel. In His loving compassion, He accepts you. Ephesians 1:6 says, "To the praise of the glory of his grace, wherein he hath made us accepted in the beloved."

My response to some rejections and put-downs was "you should have tried that before I met Jesus. Now I know who I am and whose I am, and He loves and accepts me." So those rejections and put-downs are like water rolling off a duck's back. Make these affirmations over your life daily. This is what God says about you in Ephesians 1:3–7: I am blessed. I am chosen. I am adopted. I am accepted. I am redeemed. I am forgiven. I'm believing God!

Day 7

Lady Rachel

Rachel named him Dan, for she said, "God has vindicated me! He has heard my request and given me a son." Then Bilhah became pregnant again and gave Jacob a second son. Rachel named him Naphtali, for she said, "I have struggled hard with my sister, and I'm winning!"
—Genesis 30:6–8 (NLT)

Remember, this is a story of two sisters given in marriage to Jacob. Jacob loved Rachel. But her father tricked Jacob and gave him Leah first. Then after their weeklong honeymoon, Laban gave him Rachel with the promise that Jacob would work seven more years for him. One would think that Rachel had it better than her sister because Jacob really loved her. But Rachel was jealous of her sister because her sister was having children and she was not.

Actually, both ladies envied each other. Leah envied Rachel because her husband loved Rachel. I know we shouldn't look at this with our Western eyes with our Western viewpoint. But women are women, regardless of where or when they live. There was a lot of manipulation going on.

Manipulation is a tool used to gain control and cause things to happen to benefit you and your cause. It's a trust in your own abilities and not in God's ability to provide what you need.

Rachel, you could say, chose Bilhah, her maid, to be a surrogate mother. When the first son was born, Rachel named him Dan, meaning God has vindicated her. The second son Bilhah bore, she named Naphtali, meaning "fight" because she had struggled with her sister. The word *vindicated* is a powerful word when you consider all that Jesus has done for us.

Have you ever had a person, coworker, family member, church member, or peer stand in opposition to you for no good reason, accusing you of wrongdoings, wrong motives for what you do and why you do it? You try to defend yourself, but it only builds more strife and anger. You know you're innocent and your heart is pure from evil motives. But because of their own insecurities, they hold unholy thoughts toward you. Point 1 is don't struggle with your own understanding, which will lead you to manipulating circumstances in defense of yourself. That's not of God and can only make matters worse.

I want to take a familiar passage from Psalms to show us how God will vindicate us. First, let's define the word *vindicate. M. Webster* says, "To clear of accusation, blame, suspicion, or doubt with supporting arguments or proof. To defend, exonerate."

David pleaded with the Lord to vindicate him. Psalm 26:1 says, "Vindicate me, O LORD, for I have walked in my integrity, and I have trusted in the LORD without wavering." So let's make sure we're walking in integrity and trusting in the Lord, not our own ingenuity. Let's take some pointers from that familiar passage in Psalm 37:1–7: "Don't fret or worry. Trust in the LORD. Delight in the LORD. Commit your way to the LORD. Rest in the LORD. Wait patiently for Him."

One of the hardest things for Christians to do is "stand still" (Exodus 14:13) and "wait on the Lord" (Psalm 27:14). But when we do, we'll see God's vindication. Read and meditate on these verses. These verses brought me over some hills and mountains I had to climb. God vindicated me. He'll do the same for you. He told me years ago, "Don't try to defend yourself. *I am* your defense." I know I'm a better person because of the path I had to walk. To God be all the glory.

Day 8

Lady Tamar

*When she was brought forth, she sent to her father-in-law, saying,
By the man, whose these are, am I with child: and she said,
Discern, I pray thee, whose are these, the signet, and bracelets,
and staff. And Judah acknowledged them, and said, She hath
been more righteous than I; because that I gave her not to Shelah
my son. And he knew her again no more. And it came to pass in
the time of her travail, that, behold, twins were in her womb.*
—Genesis 38:25–27

*And it came to pass, as he drew back his hand, that, behold,
his brother came out: and she said, How hast thou broken
forth? this breach be upon thee: therefore his name was called
Pharez. And afterward came out his brother, that had the scarlet
thread upon his hand: and his name was called Zarah.*
—Genesis 38:29–30

You may find this remarkable story in the entire chapter 38 of Genesis. "Hell has no fury like a woman's scorn." Judah had three sons by his Canaanite wife. He gave his first son, Er, a wife named Tamar. His first son was wicked. God slew him. Then Judah gave Tamar to his second son, Onan, to give his first son an heir. Onan would not cooperate, so God slew him. Judah promised Tamar when his third child, Shelah, became a grown-up that he would give her to Shelah. But he was not really planning to do that. He thought Tamar may have been bad luck to his sons. So he gave him in marriage to someone else. Tamar found out. Tamar set a trap for her father-in-law. From this union, she bore twins.

If you read the genealogy of Jesus in Matthew chapter 1, you will find Tamar and her two sons mentioned. Pharez (Perez) is in the lineage of Jesus. Tamar is one of five women mentioned in his lineage. Tamar, Rahab, and Bathsheba were guilty of immortality. Ruth was a gentile; and Mary, His mother, was a godly virgin.

As I read these stories of Abraham and his descendants, time and time again, I see God's grace and mercy being poured out upon His people. If He hadn't shown them grace and mercy, we would have never received the promise He made in Genesis 3:15. God had a plan. He reiterated that plan to Abraham, Isaac, Jacob, and to many other leaders in that family down through the ages.

Jacob (Israel) prophesied to all his sons when he was dying, and this is part of what he said to Judah.

> The scepter or leadership shall not depart from Judah, nor the ruler's staff from between his feet, until Shiloh [the Messiah, the Peaceful One] comes to Whom it belongs, and to Him shall be the obedience of the people. (Genesis 49:10 AMP)

Judah is the specific son, the tribe of Israel through whom Jesus would come. As you read through the history of the Israelites, keep your eyes on Judah. There will be opportunities to see how God preserves this tribe. God had a plan to redeem mankind, whom He loved, back to Himself. Therefore, over and over again throughout history, He provides grace and mercy. His Word was out, and He must honor His Word. Psalm 89:34 says, "My covenant will I not break, nor alter the thing that is gone out of my lips." This sounds like how He has dealt with our shortcomings, our deceitful, disobedient hard-heartedness and immoral acts.

Remember, if you belong to Him, it was not because you were so good; it was by grace that you're saved (Ephesians 2:8). God's unmerited favor saved you from judgment and delivered unto you salvation. It did not matter what you have done. Don't let yourself or anyone else hold over your head what you have done. At the same time, you have no right to point a finger at someone else. In fact, we should intentionally and on purpose be extending grace and mercy to others even as they mess up as Christians.

We were all a wretch undone. Furthermore, there was nothing you could have done to obtain salvation. His grace did it. The next thing is God has a plan for your life too. Jeremiah 29:11 (AMP) says, "For I know the thoughts and plans that I have for you, says the Lord, thoughts and plans for welfare and peace and not for evil, to give you hope in your final outcome."

Just as He had a plan for Jesus to enter this earth and provide salvation, He has a plan for you as well. He has been orchestrating times and events to get you to where He wanted you. Some plans, you may have cooperated with, and some you may not have. When you go to heaven, you will live a blissful life. If you avail yourself to His plans, you will live a fulfilled, joyful, and good life here on earth.

As you draw closer and closer in relationship with Him, His plans will become clearer and clearer. Listen to what Psalm 32:8–9 says to us in the TPT.

> I hear the Lord saying, "I will stay close to you, instructing and guiding you along the pathway for your life. I will advise you along the way and lead you forth with my eyes as your guide. So don't make it difficult; don't be stubborn when I take you where you've not been before. Don't make me tug you and pull you along. Just come with me!" (Psalm 32:8–9)

Let's just say, "Yes, Lord, to Your will and Your way. Not my will, Lord, but Your will be done." And obediently follow through. Surrender those areas you've been holding back and following your own way or intellect.

Day 9

Lady Shiphrah and Lady Puah

*Then Pharaoh, the king of Egypt, gave this order to the
Hebrew midwives, Shiphrah and Puah: "When you help the
Hebrew women as they give birth, watch as they deliver. If
the baby is a boy, kill him; if it is a girl, let her live."*
—Exodus 1:15–16

Pronunciation of Shiphrah is *shif-ruh* and Puah *pew-uh.*

Joseph brought his family to Egypt because there was a famine in the land. There were about seventy people, including his father Jacob (Israel), his brothers, and their families. By the time this generation had died, the Israelites had grown to a huge number that intimidated the then Pharaoh. This king tried different tactic to try to maintain population control. Read Exodus chapter 1.

I like the fact that God will either foil the plans of the devil or use His plans against him. Pharaoh wanted all the boy babies killed at birth. History repeated itself when Jesus was born. But again, it did not stop God's plan. These midwives, Lady Shiphrah and Lady Puah, were very courageous ladies. The scriptures said they feared God. The word *feared* does not mean they were afraid of Him. But even though they were probably born into slavery, they were taught about God, and they held on to their godly fear (reverence, love, and respect).

Sometimes we find our lives in some tough situations maybe due to our own makings. Don't count God out when you can't see what He is doing on your behalf. Don't allow doubt and disbelief to set in and turn back to the world and start doing and acting worldly. No! God is yet on the throne. When you don't understand why things are happening to you, dig your heels in and say, "Lord, I'm trusting you." Be like the three Hebrew men in Daniel 3:16–18 (paraphrased): "We know our God is able to deliver us, but if not, we will not bow to your image."

These ladies were in a pickle. They knew Pharaoh could have them killed. But they chose to do what pleased the Lord. God rewarded them by giving them families of their own. When Pharoah questioned them, they gave him some lame story that the Hebrew women delivered faster than the Egyptian women. When they got to them, the baby was already born.

Standing for what's right may sometimes get you in trouble. But let's stand like Peter and John in Acts 5:29, "But Peter and the apostles answered, 'We must obey God rather than men.'" When we worshipfully revere and love the Lord above anything and anybody, we are choosing to turn away from evil. It will affect the decisions that we make. It won't be so easy to casually walk in sin. We'll begin to hate what God hates and love what He loves.

> You can avoid evil through surrendered worship and the fear of God, for the power of his faithful love removes sin's guilt and grip over you. When the Lord is pleased with the decisions you've made, he activates grace to turn enemies into friends. (Proverbs 16:6–7 TPT)

Think on this. What is keeping you from walking faithfully in reverential fear of the Lord? What compromises are you making to please your flesh or somebody else? Do you hate sin? Are you walking in the reverential fear of the Lord? Psalm 111:10 (NLT) says, "Fear of the LORD is the foundation of true wisdom. All who obey his commandments will grow in wisdom. Praise him forever!"

Day 10

Lady Jochebed

The woman became pregnant and gave birth to a son. She saw that he was a special baby and kept him hidden for three months. But when she could no longer hide him, she got a basket made of papyrus reeds and waterproofed it with tar and pitch. She put the baby in the basket and laid it among the reeds along the bank of the Nile River.
—Exodus 2:2–3 (NLT)

And Amram's wife was named Jochebed. She also was a descendant of Levi, born among the Levites in the land of Egypt. Amram and Jochebed became the parents of Aaron, Moses, and their sister, Miriam.
—Numbers 26:59 (NLT)

Pronunciation of Jochebed is *jahk-uh-bed.*

So often, we think things are coincidental, but if you look closely, you'll see the handiwork of God. Read verses 2 to 9 of Exodus chapter 2 and watch how God unfolds this event right under Pharaoh's nose.

Let me go back to where Pharaoh commanded hard taskmasters to make the work so hard that he hoped the husbands would be too tired to copulate with their wives and conceive children.

This was the first attempt at population control. Well, they multiplied anyway. Those husbands were probably looking for stress relievers. Can you see God strengthening them because He had a plan?

We saw how God used the two midwives to further His plan in last week's blog. So now we come to Jochebed, wife of Amram. She conceived and saw that the baby was special. Every mom thinks that their baby is special. So what did she see? God showed her that this one was different, and she probably felt in her heart that somehow God had His hand on his life.

If you're trying to hide your baby boy, like all the mothers were doing, why on earth would you put him in a little boat and float him down the river? You're trying to hide him, not put him out in the open. I know you see God at work. Okay, so she may know Pharaoh's daughter's habit of going down to the river to bathe. I wouldn't have thought in a million years that the princess would take him as her own, name him Moses (Moses's mother nursed him until he was weaned), and take him into the palace of the man who wanted all Jewish boy babies to be killed and expect him to survive. Who does that! After all, there was a lot of antisemitism going on. Why would you think that this unmarried woman would want a baby? A Jewish baby? Oh my goodness, you know God is orchestrating all that. Grace and favor personified!

So what is your point, Ms. Helen? Open your eyes and look again at some things in your life that you thought just happened by coincidence. I began to see early on in my Christian walk that it had to be God going ahead of me preparing the way. Much of it was before I was born again. My parents prayed for me. I made some young dumb mistakes. But God!

I won't get too personal nor too detailed. But here are some examples. As a teen preparing to go to college, trying to get to a place in downtown Dallas to apply for a job, I got in the car with a total stranger. But God! I did it again when my brother and I had car trouble. I got in a car that was headed the way I needed to go home to get help. But God! I'm looking back at these things after I got saved. I'll share one more. Maybe you can relate to some of this and see God's hand on your life.

I came looking for a job as a speech therapist, straight out of college at the age of twenty-two. This was in 1970. This is early on when schools were desegregating. It never dawned on me that here I am, this little negro child going to ask a predominately White school, which was just in the beginning stage of integrating, that they would accept me to teach their children how to talk. I walked out of that interview with the superintendent and a principal, knowing within myself I had the job. I didn't even follow up on other leads. Was it timing? Was it my skills? Or was it God's hand on my life? I prefer the last one.

There are so many more times and events that I know God was orchestrating my life. I didn't know this at the time, but God reminded me after I got saved and drawing near to Him.

Life hasn't been all peaches and cream. But He has been there, sometimes quietly doing His thing—sometimes not so quietly. He was there all the time. Thank You, Lord!

Day 11

Lady Miriam

Then Miriam the prophet, Aaron's sister, took a tambourine and led all the women as they played their tambourines and danced. And Miriam sang this song: "Sing to the LORD, for he has triumphed gloriously; he has hurled both horse and rider Into the sea."
—Exodus 15:20–21 (NLT)

Read Exodus 15. Read Numbers 12:1–16.

Miriam is Moses's sister. She first appears on the scene in chapter 2 of Exodus. She was sent by Jochebed, her mother, to see what would happen to baby Moses when he was floated down the river. The princess sent her to find a Hebrew woman to nurse him. She brought his mother.

Then Miriam appears again in Exodus 15 after the Israelites crossed safely through the Red Sea. Miriam picks up her tambourine and leads the women in praise and worship. Miriam wasn't afraid to dance and shout for the goodness, mercy, and kindness of the Lord. Praise and worship are appropriate responses to what God had done for them by delivering them out of enslavement and bondage. What about today? Is praise and worship an appropriate response to God for delivering you and me from the bondage of sin? We should lift our voices in adoration for all that God has done for us. It's good to praise Him at the church house, but is that the only time we should praise Him? I wager a bet. If you don't praise Him at home, then neither will you praise Him at church. He's worthy to be praised. Singing and giving God praise will lift you out of your troubles.

Now there is another event involving Miriam in the twelfth chapter of Numbers. Moses is leading the children of Israel through the wilderness. Along the way, Moses married an Ethiopian Cushitic woman of African descent. His older siblings, Prophetess Miriam and High Priest Aaron, criticized Moses. There is no law at this point against marrying a person from another race. After all, Moses's first wife was a Midianite. So are they really opposed to him marrying this woman? Do they have another motive? Or is their jealousy manifesting? What they had to say had nothing to do with whom he married. They said, "Hath God only spoken by Moses? Has He not spoken by them too." They were questioning Moses's authority.

I have observed God calling several members of the same family into ministry. And one of them may serve as pastor over the others. Sometimes because of our familiarity with the pastor, we may fail to give that pastor the honor and respect due him or her. We must be careful in that respect even if we think they are wrong about something. We must lay it at Jesus's feet.

Moses did not even defend his decision. The Bible says he was the humblest man on earth. One translation uses the word *meek*. But God heard them. My pastor often says, "He's the unseen listener to every conversation." God set them straight.

I also see some pride being exhibited by these two. "Hasn't the Lord spoken to us also?" God said (paraphrased), "I'll speak to a prophet indirectly through visions and dreams. But to My servant Moses, I speak directly, face-to-face." So Miriam became leprous for seven days. So why was Miriam punished? Some say because she initiated the conversation. Perhaps because she was the oldest or because she was a prophetess challenging Moses, the prophet. One commentary suggested that Aaron wasn't punished. Being the high priest, he would not be able to serve the people for seven days. He suffered by watching his sister suffer. That really got their attention. They were quiet after that. Miriam is only mentioned again when she dies.

Did you notice Moses did not gloat, saying she got what she deserved? Being the humble person he was, he quickly interceded for her. When people come against you, do you pray for them?

That is one of the things Jesus told us to do in Matthew 5:43–44. Instead of praying, there are a lot of criticism and judgmental attitudes that go on in our churches today. Let's avoid those kinds of conversations. Let's put on a little humility. Pray one for another.

Day 12

Lady Deborah

Read Judges chapters 4 and 5.

Israel has been dominated by King Jabin for twenty years. God had turned them over to this king because of their sins. They went after other gods. But when they cried out to Him, He came to their rescue. God raised up a prophetess named Deborah. She sat under a tree and judged the people. God will raise up whomever He will to accomplish His plans. He is no respecter of persons.

Deborah, being the mouthpiece of God, sent for Barak. The Lord told him to take ten thousand men from Naphtali and Zebulun to fight against Sisera. Barak refused unless Deborah accompanied him. I couldn't understand why he refused if he trusted her when she said, "The Lord said." Looking back in Israelites' history, often they would take something (the Ark) that represented God's presence. Maybe she represented God's presence to him. However, she warned him that a woman would receive the honor of defeating the enemy.

In verse 14, Deborah told Barak he would have the victory because the Lord would go ahead of you. That really blessed me because many times in scripture, when Israel was cleaning out the promised land, the Lord told them He was going ahead of them. I'm also reminded that when they were traveling through the wilderness, He went ahead of them in a pillar of cloud leading the way.

As people of a better covariant, He goes ahead of us to prepare the way for us. He clears the way for us if we trust Him. Sometimes things happen in our lives where He closes a door we thought was open. He removes obstacles in our way. Events take place, and sometimes we're disappointed. But if we hold on and continue to trust Him, we'll see how that actually worked out for our good. That was Him.

There is so much richness to this story, so I'm going to jump to Deborah's song (chapter 5) where she talks about those tribes when certain ones did not come out to help fight the battle. They all had their excuses.

In chapter 5:15–16, she said the tribe of Reuben was indecisive. What makes a person indecisive? Fear and insecurity. These are demons you must resist. You must know who you are in Christ and be confident in Him. You're not meant to fight a battle alone. You're right; you can't win in your own strength and power. Paul said be strong in the Lord and in His mighty power (Ephesians 6:10). Some people need to be delivered from indecisiveness and insecurity. Gilead and Asher did not lift a hand to help.

Our combat is not physical like these battles in the Old Testament. Our battles are spiritual. But many times, we offer excuses as to why we don't respond to the battle cry. Every Christian is called to help further or build the kingdom of God. Many Christians will not open their mouths to tell someone about Jesus or that Jesus loves them just the way they are. Sinners don't need you to be their judge or criticize them. They need to know God accepts them and you do too.

They need genuine love.

God, our world is in such a mess today. People are believing all kinds of crazy stuff. I read in 1 Kings where God sent a lying spirit to some prophets. I think He has sent one to plague this world today. But I believe the universal church, body of Christ, is being held responsible. We have not and are not doing what He told us to do in Matthew 28:19–20. I know there are some people doing it, but are you? Who have you led to Christ? How often have you told someone about Jesus? You must tell them more than just telling them to go to church.

Don't be like the tribes of Gilead and Asher and simply stay home. The great commandment is not just to the preachers. We're all disciples. So He told us all to go.

People say, "I want to hear God say, 'Well done, thou good and faithful servant.'" What have you done for the kingdom for Him to say that?

Day 13

Lady Jael

*But Sisera fled away on foot to the tent of Jael, the wife of
Heber the Kenite, for there was peace between Jabin the
king of Hazor and the house of Heber the Kenite.*

—Judges 4:17

Read Judges 4:18–21.

Deborah's prophecy in verse 9 was fulfilled by Jael. Judges 4:9 (NLT) says, "'Very well,' she replied, 'I will go with you. But you will receive no honor in this venture, for the LORD's victory over Sisera will be at the hands of a woman.' So Deborah went with Barak to Kedesh."

Jael was living out her destiny. God had chosen her for such a time as this. It wasn't a coincidence that she and her husband moved to this place and on the very road that Sisera would travel trying to escape. It was a setup.

She fulfilled her destiny by using what was in her hands. She courageously defeated the Lord's enemy. She didn't have to do it. She and her husband were in good standing with the wicked king who had oppressed God's people, the Israelites, for twenty years. She chose to align herself with the one and only true and living God.

What is your destiny? God has a purpose and a plan for your extraordinary life (Jeremiah 29:11). Are you living with purpose, on purpose? Will you be ready when He calls on you to fulfill His purpose for your life? There are and there have been circumstances in your life that have prepared you for a future destiny or purpose. All of us have been chosen in Christ before He made the world (Ephesians 1:4).

We struggle sometimes with where we are in life. We struggle with some of our life choices, but I'm convinced that God had a purpose and a plan He was preparing for us to fulfill.

Resist the struggle and look to see what God is doing and what he is preparing you for. He will reveal to you His plans and purposes if you cling to Him, get to know Him intimately, and wait on Him. He wants you to know. As you seek Him wholeheartedly, you'll begin to discern what He is doing in your life.

Don't think for a second that He is not busy orchestrating your life. If you look for Him, you will find Him. Don't be afraid of what He has chosen for you to do or to be. He has your best interest at heart and, at the same time, uses you to be a blessing in someone else's life. He wants your life to be impactful to the lives you will touch. You are touching someone else's life whether it's for good or bad. He is an amazing God!

Day 14

Lady Delilah

*And it came to pass afterward, that he loved a woman
in the valley of Sorek, whose name was Delilah.*
—Judges 16:4

Read chapter 16 of Judges. Most people have heard or read the story of Samson and Delilah. If not, you'll find the story in the chapter mentioned above. The narrative says Samson loved Delilah. It does not say she loved him. We should not be upset with Delilah. She only did what she does. She made no pretense that she cared about Samson. Chances are that she was a prostitute.

Samson did not use good judgment when it came to his personal life. If only Samson had learned what Solomon, many years later, taught in Proverbs about sexual sins and the seductress woman (Proverbs 5:3–10). However, that's no excuse. The law had explicitly spoken about getting involved with foreign women. Delilah was bribed by the Philistines with many silver coins. She was probably used to being paid for her services. She had no allegiance to God nor to doing what's good and right.

What does this say for us women of today? This brings to my mind what the Lord said in Matthew 16:26: "What is a man profited, if he shall gain the whole world, and lose his own soul? or what shall a man give in exchange for his soul?" After reading and pondering the scriptures previous to this one, I realized Jesus was encouraging the disciples that if they were going to truly follow Him, they must take up their cross and follow Him. Then He says what are you going to profit if you gain all the wealth in the world yet lose your soul. What are we selling out to today? What are we exchanging for our soul?

Some women are choosing sexual sins over doing things God's way. I'm talking about professing Christians. I'm talking about women who say they've accepted Christ but are habitually living in sin. Delilah was a sinner. She did what sinners do. Sinners today do what sinners do. They sin. But professing Christians are admonished to *flee* fornication, *flee* youthful lust. Every woman should have her own husband and every man his own wife.

Still talking about professing Christians, that's the sacrifice of bearing or taking up your cross. You learn to say *no* to your flesh and its evil desires. It's dying to the flesh and living unto Jesus Christ.

It's my understanding that the Bible is written to Christians for Christians. Look at what it's telling New Testament Christians to do and not to do. So that tells me that Paul and others saw Christians doing some things they shouldn't be doing. My point is, don't be so quick to say a person must not be a Christian if they're doing this or that. I don't know a person's heart or soul. And neither do you. God knows, and Jesus said He would reward according to what you've done in this body.

Another point is that you're walking a mighty thin line when, say, you're a Christian but habitually walk in sin. Don't die in your sins! You may not end up in the place where you think you will. I wouldn't test God in that way.

Another thing, how important is material wealth to you? Are you willing to compromise Christian values to obtain wealth? Are you forfeiting your time with the Lord because you're too busy going after material wealth. For what are you giving up your soul! Pause and think about it.

Day 15

Lady Naomi

The man's name was Elimelech, and his wife was Naomi. Their two sons were Mahlon and Kilion. They were Ephrathites from Bethlehem in the land of Judah. And when they reached Moab, they settled there. Then Elimelech died, and Naomi was left with her two sons. The two sons married Moabite women. One married a woman named Orpah, and the other a woman named Ruth. But about ten years later, both Mahlon and Kilion died. This left Naomi alone, without her two sons or her husband.

—Ruth 1:2–5

Read the book of Ruth chapters 1 to 4.

We know that God brought a famine upon the land of Judah because of their repeated return to idol worshipping. We can only speculate as to why God allowed Elimelech and his two sons to die in Moab. It appears that Naomi continued to serve God even though she was in a foreign land. However, it all works to further God's divine providential plan to redeem mankind. Naomi may have missed a step in, thinking that God had opposed her, and she called herself bitter.

Most bitter folks I know generally turn away from God if they blame Him for their troubles. But Naomi continued to look to Him and even taught her daughters-in-law about Him. That's a lesson for us. When troubles and hardships come our way, don't turn away from God but run to Him all the more. We don't always understand why things happen, but if we just hold on regardless, He'll eventually turn things around for us. He'll bring a miracle out of our mess.

Won't He do it!

I'm impressed with Naomi. She could have been the mother-in-law from hell! They do exist, you know. She could have thought those foreign women were not good enough for her sons. She could have blamed the ladies for her sons' death. She could have blamed her husband and became a bitter widow. She did none of that! How do we know that?

> Then Naomi heard in Moab that the LORD had blessed his people in Judah by giving them good crops again. So Naomi and her daughters-in-law got ready to leave Moab to return to her homeland. With her two daughters-in-law she set out from the place where she had been living, and they took the road that would lead them back to Judah. But on the way, Naomi said to her two daughters-in-law, "Go back to your mothers' homes. And may the LORD reward you for your kindness to your husbands and to me." (Ruth 1:6–8)

What caused these young ladies to want to leave their own people and their gods to follow Naomi back to her hometown and to her God, a place where they would be strangers and foreigners? If she had been the bitter mother-in-law from hell as soon as their husbands died, they would have gotten as far away from her as they could. So what kind of mother-in-law was she? Naomi was full of love and kindness. When you show love and acceptance, people will want to be around you. Even little children perceive when you love and accept them.

Nobody wants to just be tolerated. People see through that facade. Naomi genuinely loved these women. They knew it, and they loved her. This type of love is described in 1 Corinthians 13:4–8. Please read it here from The Passion Translation (TPT). Are you measuring up?

Love is large and incredibly patient. Love is gentle and consistently kind to all. It refuses to be jealous when blessing comes to someone else. Love does not brag about one's achievements nor inflate its own importance. Love does not traffic in shame and disrespect, nor selfishly seek its own honor. Love is not easily irritated or quick to take offense. Love joyfully celebrates honesty and finds no delight in what is wrong. Love is a safe place of shelter, for it never stops believing the best for others. Love never takes failure as defeat, for it never gives up. Perfect Love never stops loving. It extends beyond the gift of prophecy, which eventually fades away. It is more enduring than tongues, which will one day fall silent. Love remains long after words of knowledge are forgotten. (1 Corinthians 13:4–8 TPT)

Day 16

Lady Mrs. Lot

But his wife looked back from behind him,
and she became a pillar of salt.

—Genesis 19:26

Read Genesis chapter 19 and Luke 17:32.

The Lord sent His angels and rescued Lot, his wife, and his two daughters. He then destroyed the wicked cities of Sodom and Gomorrah. The angels gave them an explicit command not to look back. But you know the story—Mrs. Lot looked back. You also know what happened to her. If not, look in Genesis 19.

To be honest with you, Lot was hesitant to leave, so the angels grabbed them by the hands and had to practically drag them out. They wouldn't leave them nor destroy the city until Lot was out because Abraham had interceded for them. God answers our prayers of intercession. Sometimes we can get too comfortable living like the world. When the Holy Spirit convicts you, there may be a struggle to turn away or leave a sinful situation in your life.

This reminds me that shortly after I got saved, I continued with some worldly ways. But the conviction of the Holy Spirit came upon me. One by one, I began to let those things drop. The danger in ignoring the Holy Spirit is that your heart becomes hardened or calloused, and you won't be able to hear the Holy Spirit. You don't want your heart to become hard like a pillar of salt.

Today, at an alarming rate, people are declaring their allegiance to Christ but want to continue with their old lifestyle. Jesus says you're not fit for the kingdom, meaning you won't be of use to the kingdom. Luke 9:62 says it perfectly. I want you to see it in KJV and TPT.

> And Jesus said unto him, No man, having put his hand to the plow, and looking back, is fit for the kingdom of God. (Luke 9:62 KJV)

> Jesus responded, "Why do you keep looking backward to your past and have second thoughts about following me? When you turn back you are useless to God's kingdom realm." (Luke 9:62 TPT)

Have you seen people try to witness for Jesus but their lifestyle is questionable? Sometimes that's why people won't witness or tell someone about Jesus because there are some worldly ways you don't want to give up. Furthermore, you don't want to be called into question about them. But sinners will remind you of what you're doing if you try to correct them or tell them about Christ. Then there are people who have failed to develop their relationship with the Lord; so they, being influenced more by the world's philosophy of life, believe the way they are living is okay, even though the Holy Spirit may be giving them opportunities to change. Instead, they ignore the unctions from the Holy Spirit. That person is not useful to the kingdom.

There are dire consequences for Christians who are caught up in the world's way of thinking. Walking in sin will not only affect you and your future but also those around you in ways you may not even begin to see. Please believe the Word. "The wages of sin is death" (Romans 6:23). Death is destructive to you and your family. Plus, it comes in many ways such as divorce, financial loss, addictions, disobedient children, physical death of you or family, sickness and disease, etc. However, I'm not saying if you're sick, it's because of a sin you've committed. Sickness is a by-product of this fallen earth due to sin committed by Adam and Eve. But your lifestyle can open the door to destruction on you and those you love.

The Lord, through Moses, told the Israelites they could choose life or death. What they chose would affect their children. This principle applies to us today.

Deuteronomy 30:19 says, "I call heaven and earth to record this day against you, that I have set before you life and death, blessing and cursing: therefore choose life, that both thou and thy seed may live." Those are things that can happen in this life. But in the life to come, being a child of God, you'll miss out on some rewards that we often take too lightly. I don't know about you, but I don't want my works to be burned up as I appear before the judgment seat of Christ (1 Corinthians 3:13–15). Also, I want to hear "well done, thou good and faithful servant" (Matthew 25:21).

Day 17

Lady Ruth

Read Ruth chapter 1.

There are two books in the Bible that bear the name of a woman—Ruth and Esther. I've read these books, but I'm thankful and ecstatic for the opportunity to study them more closely and see what the Lord will reveal to us. I do hope you will take the time to read them.

The book of Ruth opens with a narrative about a Jewish family who moved to Moab. There was a famine in their land of Bethlehem-Judah. After the death of Naomi's husband and her two sons, she decides to return to Bethlehem-Judah. She heard that the famine was over.

Is it ironic that Naomi's husband led his family away from a place whose name means "house of bread"? Is it a coincidence that this story mainly takes place in the town where Jesus will be born? When you read the story, you'll see so many parallels to His birth and life. As we move on with the story, we realize that sometimes, God will call you out of your comfort zone to accomplish what He needs to accomplish in and through your life.

In this story, Ruth is being called out of her comfort zone, away from the life and customs with which she is familiar to go and live in a land where she will be considered a foreigner unfamiliar with their customs. But she has such a strong calling or knowing inside her that those things don't really matter. Sometimes a calling will supersede the dangers that may lay ahead or the oppositions you may face. At that point, you "set your face like flint" (Isaiah 50:7) and move forward, trusting God that whatever comes, He's got your back.

Both Jesus and Paul set their faces to go to Jerusalem even though they were warned by the Holy Spirit that opposition and suffering awaited them there (Luke 9:51, Acts 20:22–24). Both men, as was Ruth, were determined in their hearts to complete their assignment.

I admire Orpah, Ruth's sister-in-law, because she didn't try to go along because Ruth was going. That was not her assignment. She would have been most miserable. Don't try to do what someone else is doing because it looks good or easy. At the same time, don't hold back because people may think you're trying to do what someone else is doing when you know in your heart it's what you're called to. I believe your assignment will not look like the other person's once you throw yourself into it.

Question? Do you know what your calling or assignment is? Is it important for you to know? Are you seeking the Lord to find out? Do you think it's too late to find out? Never! As long as there is breath in your body, you can know and accomplish it. You may ask, "How do you know if it's for you to do a certain thing?" That's simple, yet it can be complicated. First, you must have a relationship with the Lord and hear Him. Relationship trumps religion. Then you ask Him what would He have you to do. What is His plan or assignment for you?

Please know you were born with a blueprint for your assignment inside you. That's one reason why building a relationship with Him is so, so, so important and necessary. If you don't have a vibrant relationship with Him (spending quality time, talking, and listening), then all you have is a dead religion. Most or a lot of people have never sought the Lord about their assignment. Some die and go to heaven not knowing for sure why they were born or allowed to live on this earth.

Then some may have not been able to articulate it but was doing it all the time. When you see people who have an innate ability or knack for doing something, it's probably their assignment or calling, especially if it involves being a blessing to others.

This is what God has to say about the matter! There are no exceptions. It's for everyone, even sinners.

> "For I know the plans I have for you," says the
> LORD. "They are plans for good and not for
> disaster, to give you a future and a hope. In those
> days when you pray, I will listen. If you look for
> me wholeheartedly, you will find me." (Jeremiah
> 29:11–13 NLT)

Day 18

Lady Ruth Part 2–Single-Hearted Devotion

As I continue to study Ruth and what we can glean from her, I want us to look at her loyalty and devotion to Naomi and her God. So let's look at her response when Naomi urged her daughters-in-law to return home.

> And Ruth said, Entreat me not to leave thee, or to return from following after thee: for whither thou goest, I will go; and where thou lodgest, I will lodge: thy people shall be my people, and thy God my God: Where thou diest, will I die, and there will I be buried: the LORD do so to me, and more also, if aught but death part thee and me. (Ruth 1:16–17)

I know this passage is very familiar because we used to hear parts of it in wedding vows. Nowadays, couples write their own vows most of the time. This is really deep. Look at the commitment she is making to Naomi. This is spoken from her heart. You can almost sense (feel) her heartfelt sincerity in this vow. Think about the kind of loving person Naomi must have been to her daughters-in-law. She must have witnessed to them about her God in such a convincing way that Ruth is willing to turn away from the gods of the Moabites to the true and living God.

Ruth is declaring that she is giving her *all* to Naomi and her God. She purposed in her heart and verbalized it to Naomi.

What synonyms come to your mind when you think about Ruth's profession of loyalty? Words that come to my mind are *devotion, dedicated, vow, consecrated, committed, sanctified, wholehearted,* and *faithfulness.* As you read through this book, you will see Ruth walking out what she vowed. Ruth 2:10–11 shows us that people observed how Ruth treated her mother-in-law and were amazed. Ruth was also loving, respectful, humble, and obedient to Naomi. Read Ruth 3:1–6. Ruth trusted Naomi, and whatever she told her, Ruth was willing to do.

Ruth knew Naomi was doing some matchmaking. I can't imagine Ruth completely understanding Israel's custom of lying down at a man's feet and pulling his cover over you. But she willingly followed Naomi's counsel. The Bible tells the older women to teach the younger women. However, make sure the older woman who is giving you counsel is a godly woman who knows the Word and living it. Lastly, looking at her loyalty to Naomi, when Ruth married Boaz, Naomi became the grandparent to her son and helped to raise the child. The Word does not explicitly say it, but I believe Naomi went to live with Boaz and Ruth. Both these women were blessed with lifelong security and blessings.

So who are you loyal to? How loyal are you to the Lord, the One who has given you His all? Can He count on you to give Him your all? I love the hymn "I Surrender All."

> All to Jesus I surrender.
> All to Him I freely give.
> I will ever love and trust Him, in His presence
> daily live.
> I surrender all.
> I surrender all.
> All to thee, my blessed Savior, I surrender all.

I know, we're all a work in progress. That's why we have His Word, His Holy Spirit, and Him living inside us. His Word says in Philippians 1:6 (NLT), "And I am certain that God, who began the good work within you, will continue his work until it is finally finished on the day when Christ Jesus returns." Your job is to surrender to His leading and guiding. Give Him your all. Consecrate and dedicate your life to Him daily. He's an all-consuming fire (Hebrews 12:29). He'll burn away or off you everything that is not of His kingdom. Surrender! Be dedicated to Him in every area of your life!

Day 19

Ruth Part 3–Divine Interventions

Read Ruth chapter 3.

This story is filled with divine interventions. It's good to take note of this because if He intervened in the lives of His chosen people, it stands to reason that He is oftentimes intervening in the lives of His adopted children who are operating under a better covenant—a covenant that was ratified in the precious blood of His dear Son, Jesus.

So it's to our advantage to take note of this throughout the Bible, building our faith to recognize when He is divinely intervening in our circumstances.

Too often, something good happens in our lives that we know we didn't cause it to happen, and what do we say? "Boy, I was lucky." Or we'll think things are just coincidences. Are they? Also, we sometimes think it's our ingenuity, our intellect, or our ability that bring about our success. We take the credit, failing to see God's handiwork. Therefore, we fail to give Him the glory. Yes, He gives us abilities, but it all comes from Him. Maybe we need to ask God to open the eyes of our understanding so we see things from His heavenly perspective (Ephesians 1:18, Isaiah 55:8–9).

God is always at work all around us. He watches over us, and you'll never catch Him sleeping on the job. Look at Psalm 121:1–8. We love to quote it. At one time, I had it memorized and recited it whenever I got on the highway or on busy streets. Take another look at it. Then check out Psalm 46:1.

From the very beginning of the book of Ruth, we see God move upon the heart of Ruth to help take care of Naomi. You can't deny that He had a hand in that. Then this really takes the cake. Ruth goes out one morning to glean behind some workers. And she just happens to end up in Boaz's wheat field, who is their kinsman redeemer. Really? I'm sure there were several fields around there she could have gone to. She knew nothing about Boaz. Naomi didn't know what field she'd go to.

So just what is a kinsman redeemer? And why is it so important to know? How does that affect us? I had an idea what this all meant but didn't have the full understanding. Therefore, I began to research it. This is what I got from the website GotQuestion.com.

> The kinsman-redeemer is a male relative who, according to various laws of the Pentateuch, had the privilege or responsibility to act on behalf of a relative who was in trouble, danger, or need. The Hebrew term (go el) for kinsman-redeemer designates one who delivers or rescues (Genesis 48:16; Exodus 6:6) or redeems property or person (Leviticus 27:9–25, 25:47–55). The kinsman who redeems or vindicates a relative is illustrated most clearly in the book of Ruth, where the kinsman-redeemer is Boaz.

There is also a prophetic piece in all this. The book of Ruth is so pivotal to your salvation and mine. Praise be to God! This is from Got Question:

> In the New Testament, Christ is often regarded as an example of a kinsman-redeemer because, as our brother (Hebrews 2:11), He also redeems us because of our great need, one that only He can satisfy. In Ruth 3:9, we see a beautiful and poignant picture of the needy supplicant, unable to rescue herself, requesting of the kinsman-re-

deemer that he cover her with his protection, redeem her, and make her his wife. In the same way, the Lord Jesus Christ bought us for Himself, out of the curse, out of our destitution; made us His own beloved bride; and blessed us for all generations. He is the true kinsman-redeemer of all who call on Him in faith.

The last thing I want to share about divine intervention and the book of Ruth is this: the child born to Boaz and Ruth is named Obed in honor of Ruth's late husband. He is also the grandfather of King David and the ancestor of Jesus. Look at God's work. He has a purpose and a plan.

Day 20

Lady Peninnah

Read 1 Samuel 1:1–7.

We always talk about Hannah and only mention Peninnah. Sometimes we look at her disdainfully because she hurt Hannah. But there is always two sides of a coin. Both ladies were hurting. Both were in a mental health crisis.

Why is Peninnah bullying Hannah? First of all, Peninnah is the second wife of Elkanah of the priestly Levi tribe. He has two wives; however, polygamy was not God's original design for marriage (Genesis 2:21–24). There is bound to be contention between the two women. There were a couple of other women in the Bible in a similar predicament. One woman was loved by the husband, and yet she was childless. The other woman was not loved yet was very fruitful. That was Leah and Rachel.

The Bible said Elkanah loved Hannah. We are reading that statement, but that is the reality that Peninnah lived. Can you imagine the hurt she felt? She welcomed every pregnancy, thinking each time that it was going to cause her husband to love her.

I see young women of today's time having child after child, unmarried, trying to get a man to love her. Love is one of the basic needs of a woman. Sometimes we set out to get it any way we can. Some women will have a baby by a married man, thinking that's the way to win him over.

But with this attitude, love is the last thing she gets.

According to one commentary, it was the culture of the day to marry a second younger wife if the first one was childless. So

Peninnah had quite a bit of ammunition to throw up in Hannah's face. She was younger and bore many children. This went on for several years.

So what is bullying? According to www.stopbullying.gov, there are three types of bullying: verbal bullying, social bullying, and physical bullying. Verbal bullying is saying or writing mean things. Verbal bullying includes

- Teasing
- Name-calling
- Inappropriate sexual comments
- Taunting
- Threatening to cause harm.

No doubt Peninnah was using at least three of these.

Bullying has become a major issue with kids, teens, young adults, and older adults. The question you may ask is, why do people engage in bullying behavior? There are several reasons. I will mention a few—jealousy, envy, low self-esteem, lack of warm loving affection in the home, to gain control, and some who are bullies who have suffered being bullied themselves.

Information on the Internet was mostly about childhood bullying. It reported that one out of five students are bullied. We know it's become a major crisis in our country. Cyberbullying or social media bullying is at an all-time high. Kids have committed suicide as early as the age of nine because of bullying. Kids come up with creative ways to commit suicide in order to avoid the pain of being bullied.

There is also bullying behavior among adults—sometimes in husband-wife relationships, coworker to coworker, boss-employee relationships, pastor-congregant relationships. It probably happens in every relationship you can name.

If you're in a physical bullying situation, of course you need to separate yourself from that situation. If it's social, like social media, block that person or group or get off social media.

If it's verbal bullying, shaming, saying hurtful and mean things, calling you names, put-downs, it would be good to separate yourself from that situation too.

Thankfully, there are a lot of things you can do naturally. For one, talk to someone whom you trust who is godly and has a spiritual connection with the Holy Spirit. You can also seek professional counseling or therapy. I would suggest a licensed Christian counselor or therapist.

Let's explore some things the Bible tells us to do. You know you have an enemy arrayed against you. You must first recognize that. The Bible tells us to submit to God and resist the devil and he will flee from you. It also tells us to pray for our enemy (someone being used by the devil), bless them, do good to them.

When dealing with put-downs, verbal bullying, don't allow it to affect you. Know who you are in Christ Jesus and stand firm in what you know. The book of Ephesians is full of affirming statements to let you know who you are in Christ Jesus. It helps to gird up your self-esteem.

Also, having an intimate relationship with the Lord where you can take anything and everything to Him is of great help to the point that what people say to you or against you will be like water rolling of a duck's back.

> So then, surrender to God. Stand up to the devil and resist him and he will turn and run away from you. Move your heart closer and closer to God, and he will come even closer to you. But make sure you cleanse your life, you sinners, and keep your heart pure and stop doubting. (James 4:7–8 TPT)

Day 21

Lady Hannah

Read 1 Samuel 1–2:11

Hannah is the first wife of Elkanah. The Bible says, "The Lord had shut up her womb" (1 Samuel 1:5). It doesn't state why the Lord did this. But the outcome led to Hannah giving birth and giving her son, Samuel, back to the Lord. And the Lord raised up the last judge of Israel who was powerful and was a prophet or priest. He was a great leader who remained faithful to the Lord all his life.

We've discussed in previous blogs how God may have a divine finger on the life of a person. We don't always understand it, but we must trust the Lord and stay in close connection with Him. Some situations may upset us. Talk to Him about it even if you are angry. He knows we may get angry with Him sometimes. But I wouldn't waste too much time there. The anger could turn into bitterness, and that will not work in your favor.

Hannah suffered many years before she cried out to the Lord. Her suffering was twofold. First, her childless condition was of great grief to her. Secondly, she had an adversary (Peninnah) who was taunting and provoking her year after year. Different translations say she was distressed. Today we would call it depressed to the point she would not eat.

I'm not even going to discuss how her husband responded. Read it for yourself. What do you think about his response?

How do you handle problems in your life whether they are people or circumstances? What's the first thing you do? How long does it take you before you, in faith, take it to the Lord? Do you tell someone else what you're going through, or do you suffer in silence? How is your self-awareness? Do you recognize when you're depressed? Or do you think Christians don't get depressed if you have faith? Be honest. No one knows what you're thinking but you and God.

If you're my age or a generation or two younger, you may have been taught "don't tell anybody about your problems, it'll just be a gossip report" or "what goes on in this house stays in this house." Also, "just pray about it." Actually, I'm a big advocate of praying about a situation. Some people think prayer is a cheap cop-out. But to me, that person who thinks that way is not praying with expectations nor listens for answers or directions from the Holy Spirit, who is our helper.

Through prayer, God may direct you to find someone to talk to whether a trusted godly friend or a professional therapist. Yes, you have to be careful or discerning on who to talk to. But prayerfully, the Holy Spirit will lead you and give you assurances on who to talk to.

After years of suffering, Hannah took her problem to the Lord. She prayed, promising the Lord she would give the son back to Him. After she had weaned him, at about the age of three or four, she took him to the tabernacle and left him with Eli. According to 2 Chronicles 31:16, a male Levite child could perform duties at the Lord's house at the age of three and up.

Day 22

Lady Michal

Read 1 Samuel 19:27, 19:12–17, 25:44 and 2 Samuel 6:16–23.

This is a difficult name to pronounce even using the YouTube pronunciation video of it that my son, Terrell, shared with me. Pretty but difficult. It has a guttural sound in the second syllable. I just thought that would be interesting to know.

Michal is the second daughter of King Saul. King Saul, at first, promised to give his first daughter to any man who killed Goliath, the Philistine giant. Well, you know the story. David killed the giant, but King Saul gave his firstborn to another man.

I know this is biblical times, but in my opinion, women were not valued by men most of the time. They were treated like property. Saul finally gave David his second daughter after David killed two hundred Philistines and brought their foreskin to Saul.

However, after David married Michal, who loved David so much, Saul was trying time and time again to kill David. He fled for his life. After a while, Saul gave Michal to another man to marry. Many years later, after David became king, David had Michal brought to him. See why I said women were not valued but treated like property? It didn't matter what she thought or felt about it.

Today, things are somewhat different because of laws. But mothers and fathers, teach your daughters to value themselves. Teach them how valuable they are to God. God loves His daughters very much. They are created in His image and likeness. As a matter of fact, all humans are. They are remarkably and wonderfully made (Psalm 139:14 CSB).

Many times, little girls grow up with a lack of self-esteem because Mama nor Daddy did not instill in them how valuable and unique they are and that furthermore, God has chosen them for a special purpose or that they lack or have low self-esteem because there was a great trauma in their lives like physical or sexual abuse.

Parents, protect your children, sons, and daughters. Surround them with your love. I'm not suggesting be paranoid but listen for God's loving guidance. Raise them up in the nurture and admonition of the Lord. Teach them who they are in Christ Jesus. Grandparents, you have a part in this too. Leave a legacy for your children and grandchildren to look up to and to emulate.

Michal was a brave and courageous woman who stood up against her crazy daddy who wanted to kill her husband. She put her life in danger by protecting her husband. Michal was not raised up in a godly home that taught her to fear God. She had her own personal gods in her house.

Also, she did not understand David's love and exuberance for the Lord. She ridiculed David when he danced in the streets with only an ephod on after successfully retrieving the ark of God.

There could be more than one reason why she did that. For one, David escaped the king's men and was gone for years. She was then given in marriage to another man. Then David had her forcefully taken from the husband she had lived with many years. We know that her husband loved her because he ran after her, crying. Then to be brought into a harem with at least two other wives, that doesn't sound like she was very special. She mocked and ridiculed David and was barren for the rest of her life.

My last point about this story is, God loves it when husbands and wives walk together in the Lord—the husband providing godly, loving leadership for his family and the wife sharing that love for her husband and the Lord, then following the godly, loving leadership of her husband. Paul described this loving relationship in Ephesians 5:21–31. The TPT explains it best.

> And out of your reverence for Christ be support-
> ive of each other in love.

For wives, this means being supportive to your husbands like you are tenderly devoted to our Lord, for the husband provides leadership for the wife, just as Christ provides leadership for his church, as the Savior and Reviver of the body.

In the same way the church is devoted to Christ, let the wives be devoted to their husbands in everything. And to the husbands, you are to demonstrate love for your wives with the same tender devotion that Christ demonstrated to us, his bride. For he died for us, sacrificing himself to make us holy and pure, cleansing us through the showering of the pure water of the Word of God.

All that he does in us is designed to make us a mature church for his pleasure, until we become a source of praise to him—glorious and radiant, beautiful and holy, without fault or flaw.

Husbands have the obligation of loving and caring for their wives the same way they love and care for their own bodies, for to love your wife is to love your own self.

No one abuses his own body, but pampers it—serving and satisfying its needs. That's exactly what Christ does for his church! He serves and satisfies us as members of his body.

For this reason a man is to leave his father and his mother and lovingly hold to his wife, since the two have become joined as one flesh.

Marriage is the beautiful design of the Almighty, a great and sacred mystery—meant to be a vivid example of Christ and his church.

So every married man should be gracious to his wife just as he is gracious to himself. And every wife should be tenderly devoted to her husband. (Ephesians 5:21–33 TPT)

Day 23

Lady Abigail

Read 1 Samuel 25:1–43.

Someone has said, "Sometimes it better to ask for forgiveness than to ask for permission." When Abigail was told by one of her servants how her husband, Nabal, responded to David's men's request for food, she moved into action. She didn't ask anyone if they thought she should do it. She didn't even consult her crazed, drunken husband. Sometimes you must take matters into your own hands. A wise woman will know when to do this.

Abigail assessed the situation very quickly. Nabal knew who David was, but he misjudged him. He wasn't thinking with a clear head, or he would have realized the blessings that could have been bestowed upon him for helping David. Having a mean and evil attitude restricts your outlook on life.

While I was trying to think on how to describe Abigail, the Holy Spirit reminded me of the Proverbs 31 wife. I knew immediately that's who she is. I was inspired, impressed, and blessed by her response to David. Proverbs 31:10–31 says it so elegantly.

A Wife of Noble Character

Who can find a virtuous and capable wife? She is more precious than rubies. Her husband can trust her, and she will greatly enrich his life. She brings him good, not harm, all the days of her life. She finds wool and flax and busily spins it. She is like a merchant's ship, bringing her food from afar. She gets up before dawn to prepare breakfast for her household and plan the day's work for her servant girls. She goes to inspect a field and buys it; with her earnings she plants a vineyard. She is energetic and strong, a hard worker. She makes sure her dealings are profitable; her lamp burns late into the night. Her hands are busy spinning thread, her fingers twisting fiber. She extends a helping hand to the poor and opens her arms to the needy. She has no fear of winter for her household, for everyone has warm clothes. She makes her own bedspreads. She dresses in fine linen and purple gowns. Her husband is well known at the city gates, where he sits with the other civic leaders. She makes belted linen garments and sashes to sell to the merchants. She is clothed with strength and dignity, and she laughs without fear of the future. When she speaks, her words are wise, and she gives instructions with kindness. She carefully watches everything in her household and suffers nothing from laziness. Her children stand and bless her. Her husband praises her: "There are many virtuous and capable women in the world, but you surpass them all!" Charm is deceptive, and beauty does not last; but a woman who fears the LORD will be greatly praised. Reward her for all she has done. Let her deeds publicly declare her praise. (Proverbs 31:10–31 NLT)

I believe Abigail was a godly woman who heard the voice of God. The words she spoke were prophetic and full of words of wisdom, words of knowledge, as well as prophecy. These are some of the spiritual gifts that can and should manifest in our lives from the Holy Spirit (1 Corinthians 12:4–11).

There are nine spiritual gifts that the Holy Spirit will impart to us if we desire them. Paul says we should passionately, earnestly desire spiritual gifts (1 Corinthians 12:31a). The nine gifts are in three categories: (1) revelation gifts, words of wisdom, words of knowledge, and discerning of spirits; (2) power gifts, working of miracles, special faith and gifts of healing; (3) the utterance or vocal gifts, various kinds of tongues, interpretation of tongues and prophecy. I won't try to explain them here. It would make this blog too long. Read them in the Word and google them. These are supernatural gifts, not something you learn. Being intimate with the Lord will open your spirit to operate in the supernatural.

In the end, she told her husband the next morning after he sobered up what she had done. He had something like a stroke, was paralyzed for ten days, and died. David sent for her and married her. This is a remarkable story. Hopefully you will read it.

Day 24

Lady Bathsheba

Read 2 Samuel 11:1–24; 1 Kings 1:11–31, 2:13–22; and 1 Chronicles 3:5.

Bathsheba was one of the most famous women of the Bible; however, not a lot is said about her. I guess you might say her life was lived in the shadow of King David. Some have said she deliberately tempted David. I see no evidence of that. The Bible doesn't say that it was a custom of David to be on his rooftop. He was supposed to be at war like all the other kings. It just happens that Bathsheba was bathing at that time, which was probably customary. Was this a coincidence? Could she object the king's desire to lay with her? What do you think would have been the consequences had she objected? Kings could do whatever they wanted to do until God intervened with judgment.

Again, we don't see much about Bathsheba's character, but a lot can be inferred. She reminds me of Abigail, a very virtuous woman. Regardless of what happened to her, she still walked with poise, dignity, wisdom and commanded respect. You know Bathsheba was deeply hurt by the death of her former husband and her firstborn child. She probably bore some blame within her heart for their deaths. Yet she submitted to David and probably came to love him. Nothing indicates that she despised him or held a grudge against him. She bore four sons, including Solomon with David.

When David was old and sickly, she went to him, intervening for her son, Solomon's rights to the throne. She was coached by Nathan, the prophet. She reminded David of his vow to her and God that Solomon would be king. You see her honor and respect for King David as she bowed before him and called him lord. I know these things were required, but there was an air of genuine respect.

When Solomon was king, she went to him. He honored her by standing and remained standing until she sat down. It's obvious that he loved and respected her. Some Bible scholars and historians believe Proverbs 31:1–9 is actually Solomon talking about how his mom taught him. And verses 10 to 31 could be a depiction of his mom. What do you think?

Godly women in generations previous to mine were women I observed who were dignified, trustworthy, and pillars of the community. Many of them lived with husbands somewhat like Abigail's husband or may have suffered abuse, yet they held high standards for themselves and for their children. Many of these ladies wore hats on Sunday and looked very dignified.

Some women of today who live in difficult marriage relationships may walk away from it. Still, others may fight the good fight of faith and stay with it, expecting God to turn things around. Each person knows their tolerance level. Whether you stay or go, follow Proverbs 3:5–6.

> Trust in the LORD with all thine heart; and lean not unto thine own understanding. In all thy ways acknowledge him, and he shall direct thy paths. (Proverbs 3:5–6)

No one knows the inside of your home but you, your spouse and God. Let God be your compass.

Day 25

Lady Jezebel

Read 1 Kings 16:31; 18:4, 13, 19 19:1–2; 21:1–25 and 2 Kings 9:7–37.

King Ahab married Jezebel, daughter of the Zidonian king. She brought to Israel all her idolatrous practices. She was wicked, cruel, revolting, and sensual. Please take the time to read at least some of the verses cited above.

What comes to your mind when you hear the name "Jezebel"? I guarantee it's nothing good. She was the personification of evil. It's really bad to have a name that's synonymous with evil. The Bible says in Proverbs 22:1, "A good name is to be chosen rather than great riches, and favor is better than silver or gold."

I was watching a Western movie. There was this man who was the richest man in the town. He owned just about everything and everybody in the town. He was known as a very ruthless and devious man in town. The people were afraid of him. He chose riches over a good name. His daughter killed herself because of her father.

Of course, you did not choose your name; your parents did. I don't recall anyone choosing to name their daughter Jezebel. That's like naming your child Satan, Beelzebub, or one of his many other names.

Is your name a good name? Have you chosen to make your name a good name? To have a good name means to have a good reputation, a good character. Now I know everybody is not going to like you. But in general, when people hear your name, what do they picture in their mind? A liar, a manipulator, someone not to be trusted, an immoral person, a brawler, mean and cruel, a busybody, peacebreaker, etc.?

Jezebel was a big liar. She lied to her husband, which caused a man's death. You can act a lie, as well as tell one. The sad thing is, people think they get away with a lie that they acted out. But just because you're not confronted about it, doesn't mean that the other person is not taking note. You're ruining your "good name" and don't even realize it. Also, God always weighs the heart #HeKnows.

I remember students getting a bad reputation at an early age. Sad to say, but teachers would warn the teacher that gets that student the next year. Sometimes that reputation would follow that student throughout elementary and high school.

God tells us in Acts 1:8, "But ye shall receive power, after that the Holy Ghost is come upon you: and ye shall be witnesses unto me both in Jerusalem, and in all Judea, and in Samaria, and unto the uttermost part of the earth."

I know in Matthew He tells us to *go* teaching and witnessing. But in Acts 1:8, He assures us that once the Holy Spirit has come upon us, we'll have power to help us with our character. He says you'll "*be* witnesses." *Be* is first-person singular continuously. So the question is, if you are a Christian, have received the power of the Holy Spirit, what kind of character are you displaying in your home, your church, your community, at the grocery store, everywhere you interact with people? Your character should be emulating Jesus. I mean, after all, you have His Spirit in you, right?

We were created in the image and likeness of God. Once we become a child of God, we are to grow into the image of His dear Son. Our character should be resembling the character of Christ. We should be a reflection of Christ. We are His light bearers. He said, "Ye are the light of the world." He was the light of the world first. The light that shines through us is His light. This is a growing process.

God had to pull my coattail when I was raising my four children. My husband was working the eleven-to-seven or three-to-eleven shift during much of that time. I was brought up in the Baptist Church where we went to Sunday school. I wanted to raise my children in like fashion. I wanted them to know and love Jesus. In the hustle and bustle of trying to get there on time at 9:30 a.m., I had to do some fussing. No matter how early or late I got them up, they still would drag their feet. Of course, I was mad going to Sunday school where I was one of the teachers. When I got to church, pretty much on time, I was all smiles as I met and spoke to the people. God said something to the effect of "what they see out here is what your children should see at home." Busted!

What do your children, your family see in you? Do they see the character traits of Christ or the character traits of that other fella?

Day 26

Lady Widow of Zarephath

Read 1 Kings 17:8–24.

Beginning with verse 1, you'll find that God had Elijah pronounce a drought upon the land of Israel because King Ahab and his wife, Jezebel, led his people into gross idolatry. Then the Lord told Elijah to go and hide himself by the brook Cherith. God told him He had commanded ravens to feed him. He drank water from the brook and ravens brought him bread and meat in the morning and evening. But then a thing happened. The brook dried up.

Then the Lord told him to go to Zarephath, a city outside of Israel and dwell there, for He had commanded a widow to feed him. This is a very interesting story—a very real event that took place in the course of Israel's history.

I get excited when I read that God spoke to His people. It excites me because I know He speaks to His children today. You don't have to be a prophet, preacher, or teacher for Him to speak to you today. He loves to have a conversation with any of His children. Of course, He speaks through His Word and circumstances. But just as He spoke to the leaders of that day, He speaks to us today. Quite often, we don't make time to listen.

Did you notice that God spoke to the widow before Elijah came to her city? See verse 9. I don't know if she fully understood, or it could be that her faith had to increase for her to follow through. I remember years ago God speaking a thing in my spirit, but it was many years later when I realized it was God. At the time, I didn't know God would talk to anyone other than clergy. But as I grew in my faith, I learned that He speaks to all of us. In the Old Testament, He most often talked to the leaders.

When I've looked at this story previously, I've focused on the widow's faith. But this time, my attention was drawn to the word *obedience*. Obedience plays a key role in the events of this story. When I think about it, her faith was seen through her obedience. We also should take notice of the other parties involved in this story.

First, Elijah was obedient in all that the Lord told him to do. If you followed his life, you would see him obeying the Lord time and time again.

Secondly, God commanded the ravens, and they were obedient. Lastly, God commanded the widow, and she obeyed. All the moving parts obeyed. If anyone or anything failed to obey, we'd be reading a story with a different ending.

Sometimes we must obey God even when it looks foolish to others and ourselves. How rational is it when you and your child are starving and you take the last bit of meal and oil to make a cake for a man you just met because he told you to do so? No doubt her spirit was stirring inside her. She recognized he was probably a man of God. His words encouraged her to trust what he was saying. Following his directions caused her faith to increase.

How many times when things looked really bad, our faith was tested and we had to stir up our faith? Although, sometimes when things have gone from bad to worse, people have turned their backs on God and walked away from Him. This can be a temptation for us. But then you realize like I have, "where am I going to go?" I've tried the world's way, and that led to disaster. The best thing to do is to trust God and do what He says.

An obedient life is far more profitable than a disobedient life. Regardless of how bad things look, stick with God and obey Him. Don't compromise your relationship through disobedience. It's not worth it. The end justifies the means. That widow would have lost her son permanently if she hadn't chosen to obey.

I need to cut this off, but there are parents who are losing their children because they are refusing to walk in obedience to God. They're following the ways of the world, which are the lust of the flesh, lust of the eyes, and the pride of life (1 John 2:16). I'm going to stop here, but there is more to be said about obedience. Lord, save the children.

Day 27

Lady Athaliah

Read 1 Kings 8:26; 11:1–3, 13, 14, 20 and 1 Chronicles 12:2, 11, 12; 23:12, 13, 21.

Evil begets evil. This is one lady that I had not heard about who had any significant activity in the Bible days. I did not know that a woman ever ruled and sat on the throne of David. I know about Deborah and Huldah as judges. This is what made me want to write about her. I wanted to see what we could learn from her.

So I found out that Athaliah was Ahab and Jezebel's daughter. The apple doesn't fall far from the tree. She was evil like her mother.

She followed her mom's examples of lying and manipulation. Jezebel influenced (manipulated) her husband, the king, to lead the people in worshipping Baal. Plus, she had all but one hundred prophets of the Lord killed. She manipulated the town of Jezreel into killing Naboth to get his property.

Athaliah did worse than her mom. She not only manipulated her husband, the king of Judah, but she also manipulated her son, the king. Then when he got killed, she went about trying to kill all the royal sons so she could sit on the throne. Many, if not all, of them were her own grandchildren. She died a brutal death like her mom. Read the story.

Did you notice that there is a behavior that both these ladies indulged in? It's called manipulation.

At its core, manipulation is a type of lying. When someone speaks falsely for the purpose of deception, he or she is being manipulative because to deceive is to manipulate someone into thinking or behaving a certain way, according to www.gotquestions.com.

I can think of several instances in the Bible where people indulged in this sin. Let's start with the master manipulator, Satan himself. He manipulated Eve by telling her half-truths to deceive her. Abraham told a half-truth when he went to Egypt. Rebekah and Jacob used manipulation to deceive Isaac. Laban manipulated Jacob to get him to marry his firstborn daughter, Leah.

There are others. You get the picture. None of these worked out very favorably for the manipulator nor those being manipulated.

Manipulation is a way of trying to control the situation to make things turn out the way you want it to. It's not difficult to be manipulative. But as stated earlier, it's a type of lying. God does not approve of His children being manipulative. It shows a lack of trust.

If you look at our world today, there is a lot of blatant lying going on today. Its purpose is to deceive and make situations go the way they want it to go. I think a lying spirit has been released upon the earth as in 1 Kings 22:23: "Now therefore, behold, the LORD hath put a lying spirit in the mouth of all these thy prophets, and the LORD hath spoken evil concerning thee."

When you, as a Christian, are manipulative, you've taken God off the throne and placed yourself on the throne. In essence, what you're doing is trying to control the situation through deception instead of letting the Holy Spirit have control. Because it's a deceptive move, you've put Satan in control. Sooner or later, it's going to blow up in your face. It's just a matter of time.

How do you avoid this dreadfully sinful behavior? The answer is, "trust in the LORD with all thine heart; and lean not unto thine own understanding. In all thy ways acknowledge him, and he shall direct thy paths" (Proverbs 3:5–6).

When you learn how much God loves you and that you're the apple of His eye, that He loves you as much as He loves Jesus, when you realize He has your best interest at heart, no matter what it looks like, that He knows everything about you and loves you anyway, then you'll learn to trust Him and wait on Him. You won't be so quick to take matters into your own hands. You'll know "God's got this."

Day 28

Lady Hadassah (aka Esther)

Read the book of Esther.

I've finished reading the ten chapters of the book of Esther. Not my first time reading it, and many of you have probably read it before too. Join me in reading it again. They are short chapters. Chapter 10 has only three verses. Women, I know the customs of these times are very controversial. But that's the way it was during that time. Down through the ages, women have suffered and sacrificed for women's rights—still to this day. Even though Queen Vashti lost her queenship, I applaud her for her courage and standing up for herself.

I was hoping to write just one blog about Esther. But to do it justice and follow the Holy Spirit, I'm having to write a part 2 after part 1.

The Jewish people have been exiled to Babylon and held in captivity because of their disobedience and idolatrous practices. God had written into law in Exodus 20:3, "Thou shalt have no other gods before me." It's kind of ironic; the breaking of this law got them thrown into captivity. And because Mordecai was being obedient and would not bow down to a ruler, it almost got a whole race of people annihilated.

I find it rather strange that God is never mentioned in this book. Yet we still see the effects of Him working on behalf of His people. As you read this book, ask the Holy Spirit to show you God's presence, power, and handiwork. Then reflect on your life and praise Him when you look at your life and you realize "nobody but God…"

Esther is an orphan raised by her cousin, Mordecai. There are two phrases that stands out in this story—one made by Mordecai, "For such a time as this" (Esther 4:14), and the other phrase uttered by Esther, "If I perish, I perish" (Esther 4:16). This first blog will center on the first phrase.

Haman had devised an evil plan to annihilate the Jewish race from the Persian Empire. But God had a different plan. Don't you just love those "but Gods." God chose to place Hadassah (her Hebrew name) in a high position—a position of power and influence. When Hadassah, aka Esther, got the news, she was faced with two choices—to do nothing or risk her own life to hopefully save others. Before she made her decision, Mordecai reminded her she may have been chosen "for such a time as this." She called a corporate three-day fast. Then she gained the courage to do what she was called to do. The Jewish people were saved, and their enemy was destroyed.

Just as God had chosen Esther to accomplish His will and His plan, He has chosen you and me. Ephesians 1:4 says He chose us before the foundation of the world. If you're in Christ, you're chosen for the advancement of the kingdom of God here on earth. Many people get saved and just want to do nothing but wait on the time they go to heaven. You've not been chosen to do nothing. You have an assignment. You're where you are for a reason. There may be a lost soul in your sphere of influence who needs to hear the Gospel— maybe someone in your home, school, job, even your church, etc. Everybody at church is not saved. And I'm not talking just about the children.

Will you say as Isaiah said, "Here am I Lord, use me"? Will you be that brave, committed, obedient individual who will step out in faith and accomplish His work? God has placed us where He wants us to be "for such a time as this." We're not here by accident. Ask the Lord what He wants you to do to serve Him.

Day 29

Lady Queen Esther Part 2

If I perish, I perish.

Go, gather together—all the Jews that are present in Susa, and fast ye for me, and neither eat nor drink three days, night or day: I also and my maidens will fast likewise; and so will I go in unto the king, which is not according to the law: and if I perish, I perish.
—Esther 4:16

In our last blog, we learned that Haman, the king's second-in-command, was plotting to annihilate the Jewish race of people. Mordecai sent a message to Queen Esther, asking her to go to the king and plead for her people. She was afraid to go at first because it was against the law. But after she, Mordecai, and all the Jewish people in Susa fasted for three days and nights, she gained the faith and courage to go before the king. She made this declaration of faith, "If I perish, I perish."

While Queen Esther was working, God was working also. The king was restless and couldn't sleep, so he had the book of the history of his reign read to him. He came across the account of Mordecai informing him of a plot to kill the king. In the meantime, Haman is planning to hang Mordecai. But to his surprise, the king ordered Haman to honor Mordecai publicly. I believe God had a hand on causing him to become restless and reading that part about Mordecai.

Esther was willing to risk her life to save her people. She gave her all. The question is, what are you willing to give up for the advancement of the kingdom so that people's lives might be saved?

The Bible is full of examples of people making similar declarations. On one occasion, Paul had this to say, "But my life is worth nothing to me unless I use it for finishing the work assigned me by the Lord Jesus—the work of telling others the Good News about the wonderful grace of God" (Acts 20:24 NLT).

On another occasion, he told the Philippians, "For to me to live is Christ, and to die is gain" (Philippians 1:21 KJV)

Our ultimate example is the Son of God: "And he went a little farther, and fell on his face, and prayed, saying, O my Father, if it be possible, let this cup pass from me: nevertheless not as I will, but as thou wilt" (Matthew 26:39 KJV).

God is looking for believers who will totally surrender to Him and carry out His will for their lives. He wants us to seek Him with all our heart. Jeremiah 29:13 (KJV) says, "And ye shall seek me, and find me, when ye shall search for me with all your heart."

Jesus informs us that to be a follower of Christ, we must give up something.

> And he said to them all, If any man will come after me, let him deny himself, and take up his cross daily, and follow me. For whosoever will save his life shall lose it: but whosoever will lose his life for my sake, the same shall save it. (Luke 9:23–24 KJV)

Things turned out well for Queen Esther and her people. They still have a holiday they celebrate today to commemorate this occasion called Feast of Purim. Things will turn out well for you if you serve Him wholeheartedly.

Day 30

Lady Mrs. Job

Then said his wife unto him, Dost thou still retain thine integrity? curse God, and die. But he said unto her, Thou speakest as one of the foolish women speaketh. What? shall we receive—good at the hand of God, and shall we not receive—evil? In all this did did not Job sin with his lips.
—Job 2:9–10

The story of Job losing all he had says very little about his wife. I've not considered this point in the past while studying this book. This time, I was studying chapter 8 where his friend, Bildad, gave his response to what Job said. Bildad jumped in immediately and began to accuse Job of having sin in his life so he was being judged by God, whereas his friend, Eliaphaz, eased into his criticism of Job.

As I kept reading, my emotions were stirred as Bildad began to accuse Job's children. He said they got what they deserved because of sin. This is what people do who have a judgmental spirit. They judge without having all the facts.

Then I thought my response was a typical emotional response of a mother. Moms are like little red banty hens who will take her baby chicks under her wings and bristle up at a would-be attacker— one that may be double her size. She'd make such a fuss that the attacker would tuck his tail and run.

By the way, where is Mrs. Job? I know she would take offense at what the man said about her children. But women did not usually sit in the company of men. I believe she would have spoken out in defense of her children had she been there.

Job is hurting and confused about all he has lost. But what about Mrs. Job? Imagine what her life is like. Job is dealing with his mental health the best way he can. He does have friends, if you can call them that, who came to rally around him. They sat with him silently for seven days. So who's with her at this time of grief? Not overlooking the material loss, but that runs pale in comparison to the loss of ten children whom she carried for nine months, gave birth to, nursed, and watched grow into fine young men and women for whom she had such high expectations. Imagine the anguish she is experiencing.

I have experienced the transition to heaven of one child. That was a hurt that only a mom can understand. I'm thankful to God for how He continues to bring me through. Furthermore, He has caused me and another grieving parent to cofound a grief support group for moms. But I must be honest, I don't know how I would fare if I'd lost more than one child at the same time. That sounds like more than I can bear.

Yes, Mrs. Job misspoke when she spoke out and said, "Are you still trying to maintain your integrity? Curse God and die" (Job 2:9). Do you not feel her pain? She doesn't sound foolish. She sounds like a wounded individual. Job spoke some wrong and arrogant things about God that He called him on the carpet about. Let's not pounce on this woman about her outburst. Let's do what the Word tells us to do:

> Rejoice with those who rejoice, and weep with those who weep. (Romans 12:15)

Hopefully, there were some women who came to her aid and maybe sat with her, cooked her a meal, cleaned her house, encouraged her to eat, supported her in her time of mourning.

Let's think about how we support someone in their time of grief. Sometimes we do need to be silent. Give them a hug. Be prayerful about what we say. Be hospitable during this time. I've learned a lot from a friend that I've watched as she supports a grieving family. She takes them items that might be needed if family gathers at your house like paper goods, water, soda, a meal for many, and a dish or two for the repass after the funeral. If she didn't bring those items, you'll probably get a sympathy card with money in it. I have learned from her and emulate what I've seen.

Although Job's wife is not mentioned again as Job was blessed with a double portion, so was she. I believe it's safe to say she bore him seven more sons and three daughters. And perhaps she saw four generations of grandchildren. Grandchildren are a special blessing to us.

Day 31

The Virtuous Woman

Read Proverbs 31:10–31.

When I first started considering whether to write about the Virtuous Woman or not, I felt a little intimidated. I knew I didn't measure up to her. But then who does! We may have some of her qualities and yet fall short in others. My mind was set at ease as I read other writings on the subject.

One thing that stands out to me is that the Virtuous Woman is a pattern for us to model, like Jesus is our ultimate model to pattern our lives by but realizing it's a lifelong process. We should always be pressing to become more like Him. It's the same as with this Virtuous Woman. She is our lifelong goal.

There are a few things in scripture that caught my attention as I looked at various translations and commentaries. One entitled these verses as "the wise wife and mother." Another said, "The ideal wife and mother." Another said simply, "A good woman." Yet another said, "A wife of noble character." Last one I'll mention is "the woman who fears the Lord." All those headings gave me a better view of the Virtuous Woman. That last one, "the woman who fears the Lord," puts a cap on them all.

I'm just going to highlight a few scriptures as the Holy Spirit leads. Please study this awesome text for yourself. A book could be written on these texts and probably has been written. That's not my purpose here.

> A capable, intelligent, and virtuous woman—
> who is he who can find her? She is far more pre-
> cious than jewels and her value is far above rubies
> or pearls. The heart of her husband trusts in her
> confidently and relies on and believes in her
> securely, so that he has no lack of [honest] gain or
> need of [dishonest] spoil. She comforts, encour-
> ages, and does him only good as long as there is
> life within her. (Proverbs 31:10–12 AMP)

King Lemuel's (who could be a reference to Solomon) mother warns him about getting involved with the wrong woman. These verses let you know not every woman will make a good and excellent wife. This is for the single woman who aspires to be a wife one day. His mom says she is more valuable and more precious than rubies or pearls. You may wonder if your husband knows how valuable you are. Well, whether he recognizes or not, God does! He holds you in high esteem as His precious daughter. Keep walking as pleasing to the Lord; it'll pay off after a while.

She says the heart of her husband confidently trusts her. She'll do him good, not harm. "He won't have need of spoil" means he won't lack financially. She won't cause her husband to be bankrupt because of overspending.

Listening to a podcast on finances today, I told my daughter how I love seeing young husbands and wives working together to manage their finances, both agreeing that sometimes they must make sacrifices to live debt free. It does my heart good to see that.

> She seeks out wool and flax and works with will-
> ing hands [to develop it]. She is like the mer-
> chant ships loaded with foodstuffs; she brings her
> household's food from a far [country]. She rises
> while it is yet night and gets [spiritual] food for
> her household and assigns her maids their tasks.
> (Proverbs 31:13–15 AMP)

This woman is a bargain hunter. She looks for the best deals and adequately clothes and feeds her household. She doesn't mind working with her hands. She is a business-minded person.

Have you heard this saying: "A man's work is from sun to sun. A woman's work is never done"? I thought about this when the verse says, "She rises while it is night." I know many wives and mothers who rise before everyone else, get breakfast started, maybe get lunches ready, etc. I used to get up throughout the night to make sure my children were covered in bed. If they made a whimper during the night, I heard it. I guess that's why I struggle to sleep nowadays. Maybe or maybe not!

I'm going to skip over some verses to make one last point. All the verses are important. Maybe there is a verse that speaks the loudest to you.

> She opens her mouth in skillful and godly Wisdom, and on her tongue is the law of kindness [giving counsel and instruction]. She looks well to how things go in her household, and the bread of idleness (gossip, discontent, and self-pity) she will not eat. Her children rise up and call her blessed (happy, fortunate, and to be envied); and her husband boasts of and praises her, [saying], Many daughters have done virtuously, nobly, and well [with the strength of character that is steadfast in goodness], but you excel them all. Charm and grace are deceptive, and beauty is vain [because it is not lasting], but a woman who reverently and worshipfully fears the Lord, she shall be praised! (Proverbs 31:26–30 AMP)

Moms, give your children godly counsel. Utilize every teachable moment. You won't have time for idleness or self-pity if you're teaching them how to care for themselves as they grow up.

Teaching them to love God and live for Him. Yes, husbands and wives should teach them, but one should not wait on the other if one is not coming up to par. You have one time around with children. There are no makeups or do-overs. You can't teach them at sixteen to eighteen what they should have learned at nine to twelve. Don't let business and ambition overshadow your responsibility to train and teach them. Teach them how to take care of the things God blesses them with while they're in your house. Then when they become adults, they'll take care of what they obtain when they leave your house.

The Word says, "They'll rise up and call you blessed." They will also rise up and remind you where you missed it.

I got pregnant in college, got married, had two handsome little boys. My mom asked me to let her raise them. She and Daddy did help out, but I told her no because if they grew up and did good, I couldn't claim that I had any part in their raising, and they would know that. If they grew up and were bad, I'd have to blame myself for not being there for them. I am thankful that with God's help they grew up to be fine young men.

I've gotten an education, had a good career that I loved. But being a wife and mom has been and still is the most awesome privilege and gift God has given to me.

Day 32

Lady Gomer

Read the book of Hosea.

Gomer was a bad girl, y'all! She was the wife of a prophet but sold herself to other men and bore children by them. I know this sounds really awful. Unthinkable! You may think, *Why did Prophet Hosea marry a prostitute?* That's a good question!

You see, Hosea was called to exemplify the relationship between God and Israel through his marriage to a harlot (Hosea 1:2). He was not called to just preach about Israel's unfaithfulness, but he was to live it out.

Hosea is the first book of the twelve minor prophets. Some of them were prophesying during the same time period. God's heart is broken as He watches His chosen people prostituting themselves to worthless gods (idols). We think what Gomer did is awful, but God uses her to show what Israel and Judah were doing. So we can't talk about Gomer without talking about Israel and Judah.

The first five books of the Bible is called the Pentateuch. Here is where God gives them the law. One prominent law is "thou shall have no other god before me." In the next twelve books, you will encounter the history of the Israelites. This gives you a firsthand look at all their infidelities and how God forgives them over and over and over again. Hosea is prophesying for about fifty years during this time period.

If you've not experienced a spouse being unfaithful, you can't imagine the hurt, the pain, the suffering, and the grief a person feels. Multiply that a thousand times to understand (but not completely) how God feels about Israel and Judah. Hosea chose a harlot because God told him to, although he probably loved her. God chose the nation of Israel long before they became unfaithful because He loved them. He also warned them time and time again.

Gomer eventually left her husband and her children. God told Hosea to go purchase her back and love her as He loved Israel. So he went and bought her for fifteen pieces of silver and barley.

When you read the book of Hosea, it really brings your spirit down somewhat. You wonder how they can be so blatantly disobedient after God has delivered them so many times. It's like they snub their noses at Him. It's one thing to slip up and sin. But it's another thing to know what God's commandments say and then decide to do the opposite of what He's said. You know God is mighty enough to squash you like a bug, yet you defy Him anyway. Is that being brave, or is it being a fool?

But guess what. People are acting that same way today. There are those who know what God's Word says today but yet choose to blatantly walk in sin.

A spiritual sister of mine said her former pastor said over ten years ago, "If God doesn't judge America, then He owes Sodom and Gomorrah an apology." If that was true over ten years ago, what would he say today? Wickedness is running much more rampant today and will continue to get worse and worse.

When I read Revelations, I saw that the more God poured out judgment upon the earth, some people repented. But there were a great number who got mad at God and sort of balled their fist up at Him. So if Revelations is the end-times book, that tells you things are not going to get better.

But God's love is so strong toward mankind He continuously tries to get man's attention so we will turn and repent. If you read the book of Hosea, you will see God pronounce judgment and turn around and speak lovingly and kindly about Israel and Judah. Now that's really going far out to command a man to marry a promiscuous woman in order to portray His love and Israel's adulterous behavior.

He continues to do that today. Scripture says in Revelation 3:20, "Behold, I stand at the door, and knock: if any man hear my voice, and open the door, I will come in to him, and will sup with him, and he with me."

Eventually, God is going to get His way. It's prophesied several times that God is going to redeem Israel in the last days when He sets up His millennial reign (Hosea 1:10–11, 2:14–23).

Actually, He has already redeemed mankind, but we have to make the decision to accept His redemptive plan. Have you accepted His redemptive plan?

Day 33

Lady Elizabeth

Please read Luke 1:5–25, 39–45, 57–80.

As we move to the New Testament, we encounter two women whom God would use to establish His kingdom here on earth. Both Elizabeth and Mary would play a key role in God's plans and purposes. In this blog, we will concentrate on Elizabeth.

Elizabeth was the wife of a priest named Zechariah. They both are descendants of Aaron. They were described as devout and obeying the commandments of the Lord. I love this couple because they both were dedicated to the Lord. They were righteous in God's eyes. There are a few people in the Bible where it says they walked with God. This could easily be said about Zechariah and Elizabeth.

It appears they never wavered even though Elizabeth suffered the disgrace of not being able to conceive and bear a child. But they kept this in prayer before the Lord. They kept the faith even until past the childbearing age. That sounds like another couple we know, Abraham and Sarah, right! God rewards faith, and He rewards obedience.

They were righteous because they obeyed the commandments. However, we New Testament Christians are deemed righteous because we are made righteous through our Lord and Savior Jesus Christ.

And of course, obedience to His word should describe our walk.

There are so many benefits to living a righteous lifestyle. There are so many promises to the child of God. One benefit to being in right standing with the Lord is having a relationship and fellowship with the Lord. This ushers in so many more benefits. I was about to say there is nothing or no relationship that can be compared to a vibrant, loving, and intimate relationship with the Lord. Just as I thought that the Holy Spirit reminded me that a husband-and-wife relationship (that is lived according to Ephesians 5:21–33) is compared to Christ relationship to the church. I may get some push back on that statement. But remember I said that's lived according to Ephesians 5:21–33.

> And after those days his wife Elisabeth conceived, and hid herself five months, saying, Thus hath the Lord dealt with me in the days wherein he looked on me, to take away my reproach among men. (Luke 1:24–25)

When I read this, I wondered why she secluded herself for five months. The Bible doesn't say. But we see her reaction in verse 25. She was overjoyed. Many times when a woman conceives a much-desired pregnancy, she can become a bit overprotective, especially if it's the first one after a long time waiting. As I think of the protectiveness of a mother, I'm reminded of this commercial where this mom was so very particular with the first child; but when the second one came along, she handed him off to a mechanic with oily hands as she searched her purse to pay him. I thought that was funny but described a lot of first-time moms.

Maybe Elizabeth wanted to get past the first trimester trying to avoid anything that might cause a miscarriage. But one thing we do see is the joy she displayed when she realized she had conceived. I look at society today and how we treat our unborn children as opposed to Elizabeth's reaction. There is so much that can be said here. I'll let you and the Holy Spirit have that discussion.

Even at six months when Mary, the mother-to-be of Jesus, comes for a visit, Elizabeth and her baby is joyful as the Lord reveals to her that Mary is the mother of her Savior (Luke 1:39–45). She is filled with the Spirit and speaks a prophetic word to Mary. There was tremendous joy in that house that day.

Elizabeth realizes that she is being favored or honored that day because she said in Luke 1:43 (TPT), "'How did I deserve such a remarkable honor to have the mother of my Lord come and visit me?" You know Elizabeth suffered disgrace for many years, endured the shame and whispers going on about her. This song came to mind by Hezekiah Walker, "God Favored Me." I'll end this blog with a portion of this song.

> This is my testimony, everybody,
> Of how God favored me in spite of my enemies.
> And if God did it for me, he'll do the same thing
> for you.
> Don't worry about your haters.
> Your haters can't do anything with you.

Listen to these words.

Love is patient, caring. Love is kind. Love is felt most when it's genuine. But I've had my share of love abused, manipulated, and its strength misused. And I can't help but give you glory when I think about my story. And I know you favored me because my enemies did try but couldn't triumph over me. Yes, they did try but couldn't triumph over me.

Day 34

Lady Mary

Please read Luke 1:26–51.

When Elizabeth was six months pregnant, the angel Gabriel paid another visit. This time he went to the town of Nazareth in Galilee and appeared to a virgin named Mary who was engaged to Joseph, a man who was a descendant of King David (Luke 1:26–27). Gabriel told her she was highly favored and the Lord was with her. He also told her she would give birth to the Son of God (Luke 1:31–33).

There are three, maybe four, things that have caught my attention. When studying the Word of God, take note of what stands out to you. It's the Holy Spirit's way of illuminating the Word to you. You'll want to meditate on them and see how you can apply them to your life. Then pray and ask the Lord to help you walk in that revelation.

The first thing is the angel telling her she is highly favored. God's favor or grace is upon her life. Grace is free, unmerited, and unearned favor. That sounds like what you and I have been blessed with if we're in Christ. Ephesians 2:8 (AMP) tells us,

> For it is by free grace (God's unmerited favor) that you are saved (delivered from judgment and made partakers of Christ's salvation) through [your] faith. And this [salvation] is not of yourselves [of your own doing, it came not through your own striving], but it is the gift of God.

Therefore, we're no longer slaves to sin. We've been set free, and we master it. Furthermore, we don't have to strive trying to make heaven our home. It's already a done deal. Hallelujah! And all of God's promises are our benefits of favor.

Verses 31 to 33 show us that Mary has been chosen to bear a Son who will be the Savior of the world. The word *chosen* stands out to me because I know that God has chosen each of us for a purpose or assignment. We were chosen before the foundation of the world according to Ephesians 1:4: "According as he hath chosen us in him before the foundation of the world, that we should be holy and without blame before him in love."

Look at how long ago He chose you. You can hardly imagine that. But you accept it by faith. He chose you to be holy, which means "consecrated and set apart for God's use" (AMP). It's time to find out your assignment.

Mary's humility stands out to me. Luke 1:38 says, "And Mary said, Behold the handmaid of the Lord; be it unto me according to thy word. And the angel departed from her."

Too many times we want to do things our own way and not humble ourselves and do things God's way. I guess we think we know better than God how to handle situations. We are so self-sufficient that we don't take the time to listen and see if what we're about to do is in the will and plan of God. We often think, *It's a good idea*, but we fail to stop and consider, *Is it God's idea?* One reason is it takes too much time to stop, listen, and find out if it's in His plan or will. Or maybe our pride in our self-sufficiency won't let us humble ourselves under the hand of God. It's my-way-or-no-way attitude!

Lastly, Mary was so excited to do the will of God that she wrote a song to the Lord expressing her joy and praising Him. If you're not excited, enthused, and passionate about what you're doing "for the Lord," don't waste your time. It's not from Him. Go back and truly find out what His will is. Then your life will be filled with joy, excitement, and exuberance to fulfill your purpose in life.

Day 35

Lady Martha

Please read Luke 10:38–42 and John 11:1–46, 12:1–3.

This week and the next, we're looking at two sisters. To me, they represent two groups of dedicated saints in the church. This week we'll look at Martha. Martha was a very hospitable person. Hospitality was probably her gift. Do you know what your gift is? Study the gifts listed in 1 Corinthians 12, Romans 12, and Ephesians 4. You may have more than one. Your gift supports your purpose or calling.

One day, Jesus and His disciples were passing through Bethany on their way to Jerusalem. Martha invited them into her home for dinner. Her sister, Mary, and their brother, Lazarus, lived with her.

Martha got busy preparing to serve Jesus and His disciples. She became frustrated and irritated because she had so much to do and her sister was not helping. She was complaining about it and asked Jesus if He did not care that her sister was not helping her. Martha represents one group of people in the church. They love to do church work. They serve on every committee in every auxiliary or several ministries. They overload themselves with church activity until they begin to complain about what others are or are not doing. They're too busy to spend time sitting at Jesus's feet. They may be sincere about their motives for doing so much. But ther. they may be motivated by the applause or recognition and praise of men (people).

Regardless of their motivation, they are missing the main thing. Their priorities are misguided. Jesus said at one point in His ministry that He didn't come to be served. He would rather have a relationship with us than for us to fill our lives with doing, doing, doing. However, church work is necessary, but if you spent time with Him, He would tell you or show you what He wanted you to do.

This applies not only to church life but also homelife. We get so busy with life that we don't have time to cultivate a healthy, vibrant, and intimate relationship with the Creator of everything, our Lord and Master. We get distracted by the cares of this world. The Lord told and warned the Israelites not to forget Him when they eat and are full, have houses and land, silver, and gold. (Deuteronomy 8:11–17). We today face the same situation. We have possessions, family, and successful jobs—sometimes more than one job. We fill our lives with so much stuff that we have to take care of that we don't have time for God or don't take time for him.

We can feel like our own hands have supplied what we have or need. The Israelites made that same mistake and forgot God.

Have you been distracted? Are you too busy to sit at Jesus's feet? Do you think it's necessary? Or are you doing all right on your own?

Day 36

Lady Mary, Martha's Sister

Please read Luke 10:38–42; John 11:1–46, 12:1–3; and Mark 14:3–9.

As I began writing about these two sisters, I said they represent two groups in the church. Mary represents the second group of dedicated saints in the church. This group hungers and thirst for a relationship with the Word of God.

Man! If all of us would be like Mary! Mary was hungry not for natural food but for spiritual food. Too many times we don't have enough hungry Christians. People seem to be satisfied with doing church work or activities. I remember Jesus once said in Matthew 4:4 (NLT), "But Jesus told him, 'No! The Scriptures say, "People do not live by bread alone, but by every word that comes from the mouth of God."'"

Martha was complaining to Jesus about her sister because Mary was not busy helping her prepare the meal for Jesus and His disciples. It's interesting how He responded. He told Martha that she was worried and fretting about many things, but look at what He said about Mary in Luke 10:42, "But one thing is needful: and Mary hath chosen that good part, which shall not be taken away from her." He said, "One thing is needful and Mary has chosen that that good part (one thing)." In Matthew 6:33 from the TPT, Jesus says, "So above all, constantly chase after the realm of God's kingdom and the righteousness that proceeds from him. Then all these less important things will be given to you abundantly."

He's talking about priorities. There are other things that are important, but they're less important than seeking Jesus, His kingdom, and His righteousness.

Let's check out Mary's priorities. Several times in the scriptures cited at the beginning of the blog, you will find Mary at the feet of Jesus. She is either listening intently to Him in Luke 10:41–42. She is loving on Him by anointing His feet with very expensive perfume, then wiping His feet with her hair in John 12:3. We find her falling at Jesus's feet in John 11:32. In Mark 14:3–9, Mark is reporting that she poured that expensive perfume on Jesus's head. She is in Bethany at Simon the Leper's house. Do you think she is kind of obsessed with Jesus?

I wish you could see my face with the biggest grin on it and wanting to say absolutely *yes*! When I grow up, I want to be just like her!

Let's search and examine our hearts. How much do we love Jesus? Are we obsessed with Him? What does that look like for us?

Day 37

Lady with an Issue of Blood

Please read Matthew 9:20–22, Mark 5:25–34, and Luke 8:43–48.

> And there was a woman who had had a flow of blood for twelve years,
>
> And who had endured much suffering under [the hands of] many physicians and had spent all that she had, and was no better but instead grew worse.
>
> She had heard the reports concerning Jesus, and she came up behind Him in the throng and touched His garment. (Mark 5:25–27 AMP)

I like the way the AMP translation described her condition. The first thing we see is that this woman had an issue. When I think of a person having an issue, I think that person has a problem with something or someone. This lady had an issue with her blood. It constantly flowed. She was bleeding and could not control it. Can you imagine how weak she must have felt? She had to be very anemic, probably needing an infusion of iron. I can't imagine dealing with a flow for twelve years.

Sometimes it's a problem today for women to have that flow each month. You can think of all kinds of problems that caused her condition. Today, many times than not, physicians can identify the problem and fix it. However, there are times they can't correct it.

She had another problem. Society considered her unclean. The Law spells it out in Leviticus 15:19–31. She was treated somewhat like a leper.

But she heard "the reports concerning Jesus." That really stood out to me. How or where did she hear the reports? Did you know you (being a layperson) could help someone's faith to develop and grow?

> How then shall they call on him in whom they
> have not believed? and how shall they believe in
> him of whom they have not heard? and how shall
> they hear without a preacher? (Romans 10:14)

I think we believe this passage in Romans applies only to ordained preachers. Suppose for a moment it could apply to you and me. Some translations translate *preacher* as *messenger*. A couple of Bible dictionaries I looked at says "to herald, proclaim, publish."

So how or where did she hear reports concerning Jesus? It could be the man who had a legion of unclean spirits.

> Howbeit Jesus suffered him not, but saith unto
> him, Go home to thy friends, and tell them how
> great things the Lord hath done for thee, and
> hath had compassion on thee.
> And he departed, and began to publish in
> Decapolis how great things Jesus had done for
> him: and all men did marvel. (Mark 5:19–20)

This man began to publish in Decapolis, meaning ten cities, what things Jesus had done for him. Do you freely and often tell people the good things Jesus has done for you?

Jesus has told us to "go tell it." Or do you think that's being too religious? I didn't say tell others about their sins. They need to hear something they don't know.

Sad to say, but sometimes we fail to recognize when the Lord does something for us. It's not just the spectacular but recognizing and thanking Him for the little things. We are too quiet, too quick to think they don't want to hear us! It's not about you. It's about Jesus!

I'm guilty sometimes of thinking they don't want to hear me, and I'm not just talking about in the church. There are times I want to tell someone about a seemingly insignificant thing God did. Then I may think, *Will they get it or appreciate what it means to me, or will it just lose its punch?* There are a few people I can share with, and they will genuinely rejoice with me.

Imagine if we shared with people we knew or didn't know, how their faith can be impacted. That lady with the issue of blood had faith before she touched Jesus because she had heard of Jesus. She believed their reports. Wouldn't it be magnificent if a person came to a difficult place in life but he or she remembered how you shared what Jesus had brought you through and it caused him or her to have faith to go through victoriously? Be willing to share your story. It doesn't have to be a major story. To God be all the glory!

Just think. If David hadn't been willing to share his story, his ups and his downs, we wouldn't have the Psalms today. Just think, we wouldn't have the Bible if the inspired men of God hadn't told theirs and other people's stories. Just think. God told the Israelites to not only tell their stories but to celebrate it with big festivals several times a year. So you see, there is nothing new about telling it. God ordains it. Start with your family and friends.

Keep a gratitude journal. That will help keep it on your mind and help you to begin to see specifically the things God does—more specific things that pertains to only you. Oh, the joy of simply knowing and saying, "God did that." Sometimes we know it, but we're not willing to tell it. Let's open our mouth and tell others about our encounters with the Lord. Be a name-dropper! Share it. Don't keep it to yourself. There is someone who needs to hear your story.

Day 38

Lady Anna

Please read Luke 2:36–38.

Not much is written about Lady Anna. Only three verses. But what we see is very impactful. I admire her so much. I know it's the move of the Holy Spirit, but I always get this warm feeling. It lights a fire within my soul when I've come across these verses. She portrays a woman totally devoted to God—a woman after God's own heart.

Anna became a widow at a very early age, still within childbearing age. I believe she chose not to remarry and have children but to devote her life to God. Eighty-four years later after her husband's death, she is still devoting herself to serve God through fasting and prayers. I know she studied the Scriptures because she was waiting expectantly for the Messiah. She not only studied the Word, but she believed it.

This woman is the embodiment of "women seeking intimacy with God." I'm not suggesting that we go live in or at the church house. I'm not suggesting that we should be there every time the church doors open nor work on every committee just to say we are serving God.

What does this kind of commitment look like today? Since Jesus has come, lived, died, resurrected, and ascended to the right hand of Father God, our bodies, if we're born-again, are now the temples of God. God resides in our temples. First Corinthians 3:16 says, "Know ye not that ye are the temple of God, and that the Spirit of God dwelleth in you?"

This woman is seeking to be in the presence of her God continuously. The temple, as well as the ark of God, represented the presence of God under the old covenant.

Today, under the new covenant, God's presence is always with us and in us. For us to seek His presence means we are seeking His manifest presence. *Manifest* means "to make known, to show forth, to reveal." God has so much He wants to share and reveal to us (Stephen Holford, NDMinistry). More importantly, He wants us to know Him, not just know about Him. To get to know Him in a deeper way is through His manifested presence. Then you'll know Him through experience. He will manifest Himself in many ways such as through anointing, revelations, dreams and visions, a knowing, highlighting his Word in your spirit, overwhelming joy, etc. We may also call these God encounters.

There are so many scriptures that witness to what I'm saying.

> For since the beginning of the world men have not heard, nor perceived by the ear, neither hath the eye seen, O God, beside thee, what he hath prepared for him that waiteth for him. (Isaiah 64:4)

> But as it is written, Eye hath not seen, nor ear heard, neither have entered into the heart of man, the things which God hath prepared for them that love him. But God hath revealed them unto us by his Spirit: for the Spirit searcheth all things, yea, the deep things of God. For what man knoweth the things of a man, save the spirit of man which is in him? even so the things of God knoweth no man, but the Spirit of God. Now we have received, not the spirit of the world, but the Spirit which is of God; that we might know the things that are freely given to us of God. Listen to the Psalmist express his longing for the Lord. This is so rich. (1 Corinthians 2:9–12)

> As the hart panteth after the water brooks, so panteth my soul after thee, O God My soul thirsteth for God, for the living God: when shall I come and appear before God? (Psalm 42:1–2)

Does not your soul burn within when you hear the psalmist express his desire, his longing for the Lord? This causes me to want more and more of God, wanting to be in His manifested presence.

> O God, thou art my God; early will I seek thee: my soul thirsteth for thee, my flesh longeth for thee in a dry and thirsty land, where no water is; To see thy power and thy glory, so as I have seen thee in the sanctuary. Because thy lovingkindness is better than life, my lips shall praise thee. Thus will I bless thee while I live: I will lift up my hands in thy name. My soul shall be satisfied as with marrow and fatness; and my mouth shall praise thee with joyful lips: When I remember thee upon my bed, and meditate on thee in the night watches. Because thou hast been my help, therefore in the shadow of thy wings will I rejoice. My soul followeth hard after thee: thy right hand upholdeth me. (Psalm 63:1–8)

What love! What love!
What is your greatest desire? What does your soul follow hard after? Ruminate (meditate on) the verses I've shared. They will spark your desire for more of Him.

> Thou wilt show me the path of life: in thy presence is fullness of joy; at thy right hand there are pleasures forevermore. (Psalm 6:11)

Day 39

Lady Herodias

Read Matthew 14:3–12, Mark 6:17–29, and Luke 3:19.

My first thought about Herodias is that she is no lady. My second thought is that she is the reincarnation (if there were such a thing) of Jezebel. She was full of evil. She didn't care who she hurt just to get what she wanted.

Like Jezebel who had God's prophets killed, Herodias had a prophet of God killed also. Herodias hated John the Baptist because he spoke out against Herod marrying his brother's wife. He spoke this publicly. Herod didn't want to kill John because he thought doing so might start a riot. He also had respect for John as a holy man.

So Herodias waited, plotted, and schemed for an opportunity to have John killed. She seized the opportunity when her daughter danced for Herod at a birthday party. He invited his dignitaries. Herod enjoyed his stepdaughter's sensuous dancing so much that he promised her anything she wanted up to half his kingdom. Now that sounds like a wild-eyed drunk man. So the girl went to her mother to find out what she should ask. Here is Herodias's opportunity to carry out her scheme.

Herodias is raising her daughter to be like her—immoral, bitter, and a manipulative woman. I know you've heard the saying "If you want to know what a young lady will be like, look at her mother." The same goes for father and son too. Young brides- and grooms-to-be have been warned to look at the family line. This observation can be very telling. But so many times young people don't heed the warning.

Parents, be aware that you are teaching your child(ren) by example much more than by words. Children trust that what their parents do is correct or the right way to live. Whatever a Bible teacher, professional teacher, or any other person teaches a child, it will be sifted through what they've learned at home.

I spoke to a group of "Upward Bound" young people years ago. This program was designed to help high schoolers make decisions that would best lead to their success in life. I never will forget what a young lady's response was as I encouraged them in making good choices. In essence, she said, "This is what my mom did, and she's doing all right." Let me just say her ambitions were extremely low, perhaps because that's all she knew. I saw a viscous cycle that she would be participating in.

The Bible commands us in Proverbs 22:6 (KJV), "Train up a child in the way he should go: and when he is old, he will not depart from it."

Proverbs 22:6 (TPT) says, "Dedicate your children to God and point them in the way that they should go, and the values they've learned from you will be with them for life."

I love this verse from both translations. This verse used to challenge me because sometimes children don't choose to go the way you think they should. But I've learned that our job is to dedicate them to God through training and also help them find their path in life that God has chosen for them. This doesn't happen through osmosis. No, you must be intentional in teaching them through example and imparting wisdom to them. The Bible is the best wisdom book.

It's not enough to take them to church. They spend one hour in church, about eight hours in school. The other fifteen hours (give or take), they are with you. Do they see what they learned at church in you? Do they see Christ in you? Do you mention God or Jesus at home? Do you sing or play Christian music at home, in the car? Find opportunities to drop His name. Let them know how much He loves them.

Day 40

Lady Syro-Phoenician Mother

Please read Matthew 15:21–28 and Mark 7:24–30.

Mothers will go to extreme measures to protect and provide for their young. A mother hen will pull her little chicks under her wings and bristle up at a dog who is much bigger and much stronger. The mother we read about in these verses is another example of a mother using extreme measures to provide for her child.

There are a couple of things I hope will be encouraging to you. First of all, Jesus doesn't do anything mindlessly. He's very purposeful and intentional about his behavior. After He finished teaching, he went to a non-Jewish region—Tyre and Sidon. Mark says He went into a house but people found out He was there. Matthew doesn't mention a house. Jesus's main mission was to the lost sheep of Israel.

But keep in mind, God told Abraham all nations would be blessed through Him. My conjecture is that this was an opportunity for other nations to receive grace. Jesus said He always does what He sees His Father do.

> Then answered Jesus and said unto them, Verily, verily, I say unto you, The Son can do nothing of himself, but what he seeth the Father do: for what things soever he doeth, these also doeth the Son likewise. (John 5:19)

When did Jesus see His Father do anything? It had to be through revelation or prophetic. He knew He had to impact someone's life in that region. After His death, burial, and resurrection, healing and deliverance were available to all nations.

Now let's look at the mother. She had a "never give up" spirit. She received four no's—three from Jesus and one from the disciples. Jesus actually never said no, but she could have received behavior as rejection. Have you ever received rejection? I certainly have, and I'm sure you have too. How does it feel to be rejected? It has a way of impairing your self-esteem, makes you feel like quitting and running away.

This Canaanite woman probably felt the same way. For her daughter's sake, she persevered. At this point in history, she had no right to expect anything from Jesus, a Jew.

If you follow the history of the Israelite people, you'll remember Canaan was the promised land for the Israelites coming through the wilderness after being delivered from slavery in Egypt. But they failed to extinguish all the Canaanites as God commanded them. Canaanites were very wicked and committed many atrocities and was under God's judgment.

So here we have a descendant of Canaan asking Jesus for mercy for her child. At first, He ignored her, that as well as the other responses were total rejections. She could have stormed off upset and her pride hurt. But she humbled herself, persisted in prayer even to the point of worshipping Him.

Oh, what a magnificent picture of the kind of faith we, His children, should walk in. If you don't receive your answer at first, don't quit. Never give up. Keep standing in faith. And most of all, worship Him with your whole heart. I love the scriptures in 1 John. I'll share them from the Amplified translation.

> And this is the confidence (the assurance, the privilege of boldness) which we have in Him: [we are sure] that if we ask anything (make any request) according to His will (in agreement with His own plan), He listens to and hears us. And if (since) we [positively] know that He listens to us in whatever we ask, we also know [with settled

and absolute knowledge] that we have [granted us as our present possessions] the requests made of Him. (1 John 5:14–15)

While we're waiting for our prayers to be answered, let's not focus on what we can see (the problem) but focus on what is not seen, His promises—the answer.

We were given this hope when we were saved. (If we already have something, we don't need to hope for it. But if we look forward to something we don't yet have, we must wait patiently and confidently.)

Be steadfast, unmovable, unshaken always standing in faith for what you believe is you're in Christ. (Romans 8:24–25)

Day 41

Lady of Samaria

Please read John 4:7–42.

It doesn't matter what you have done or how you have lived your life thus far. You could have lived a very promiscuous life. You may have been molested or raped as a child by a family member or mother's boyfriend. You may have committed one or more abortions. You may have abandoned or left your children with a relative who raised them.

Maybe you got hooked on drugs or alcohol. You might say, "You name it, I've done it." You may be ashamed and think, *I've done too much for God to save me. I'm not worthy, or I'm not good enough for Him to love me or save me.*

But I'm here to tell you that Jesus will go out of His way just to save a sinner like you. We used to sing this song, "If He has to reach way down, Jesus will lift you up." That is so true. You can't go too far down that He can't lift you up and transform your life. Let's consider this immoral woman that Jesus made a special trip just to save her.

This woman was ashamed of her lifestyle. Neighboring women despised her, treated her with contempt. Plus, she was disliked by the Jews for being a Samaritan. Her self-esteem has probably hit rock bottom.

She went to draw water in the heat of the day. The usual time for women to go draw water was early in the morning or later in the evening. Why did she choose to go in the heat of the day? Probably to avoid those respectable women who would make her feel even worse about herself.

But praise be to God, who had a better plan. She met someone who would love her in spite of her past or her present—someone who accepted her and gave her that living water that transformed her life, so much so that she testified of Him and many others became believers.

Are you willing to testify to others about the goodness of Jesus Christ? Are you willing to tell others about what He has done for you? Are you like the Samaritan woman who ran to go tell it?

Jesus was on His way to Galilee, and John 4:4 says, "And he must needs go through Samaria." According to one commentary, Jews despised Samaritans so much that they would take the longer route to get to Galilee. But Jesus had a need to go through the territory of Samaria. Jesus is not in the business of shunning or rejecting people. He will do what is necessary to get people saved.

Jesus gave this invitation to anyone who would open their heart and let Him come in.

> Look! I stand at the door and knock. If you hear my voice and open the door, I will come in, and we will share a meal together as friends. Those who are victorious will sit with me on my throne, just as I was victorious and sat with my Father on his throne. Anyone with ears to hear must listen to the Spirit and understand what he is saying to the churches. (Revelation 3:20–22 NLT)

Notice He said *anyone*. He didn't say "after you've gotten yourself cleaned up." He will take you as you are. Your job is to surrender to Him. His job is to transform you to new life. You become a new creation.

> Therefore, if anyone is in Christ, he is a new creation; old things have passed away; behold, all things have become new. (2 Corinthians 5:17 NKJ)

Day 42

Lady Sapphira

Please read Acts 5:1–11.

I'm starting this year off taking a look at Sapphira. Sapphira was a woman of the early church. She was married to Ananias. Peter asked Ananias a question in Acts 5:3: "But Peter said, Ananias, why hath Satan filled thine heart to lie to the Holy Ghost, and to keep back part of the price of the land?"

So Satan filled Ananias's heart to lie. And his wife Sapphira agreed with him and followed him. Read the passage to see what happened to them. Peter said they lied to the Holy Spirit. I'm trying not to be too hard on this couple because they had to be new converts since this is the beginning of the church age. However, God has some strong words against lying.

> There are six things the LORD hates no, seven things he detests: haughty eyes, a lying tongue, hands that kill the innocent, a heart that plots evil, feet that race to do wrong, a false witness who pours out lies, a person who sows discord in a family. (Proverbs 6:16–19)

Lying is number 2 on the list of seven things God hates, even detests. The KJV says these seven things are an abomination to Him. Let's see what the Word says about liars, ones who make it a practice to lie and deceive.

> But the fearful, and unbelieving, and abominable, and murderers, and whoremongers, and sorcerers, and idolaters, and all liars, shall have their part in the lake which burneth with fire and brimstone: which is the second death. (Revelation 21:8)

Now we may not want to admit it; but I imagine we all have, whether unintentionally or intentionally, told a lie at one time or another. We may categorize them as a little white lie or an exaggeration. Some may think it's okay and there is nothing wrong with a "little" lie. Let's revisit what Peter said to Ananias. "But Peter said, Ananias, why hath Satan filled thine heart to lie to the Holy Ghost" (Acts 5:3a). You know that Satan or the devil is a liar and the father of lies according to Jesus.

> Ye are of your father the devil, and the lusts of your father ye will do. He was a murderer from the beginning, and abode not in the truth, because there is no truth in him. When he speaketh a lie, he speaketh of his own: for he is a liar, and the father of it. (John 8:44)

Now we see why God hates and detests lying and it's an abomination to Him. I don't know that whenever we tell a lie, we're lying to the Holy Spirit or not, but I believe He is grieved when we do so because He is living inside us. Ephesians 4:30 tells us not to grieve the Holy Spirit and lying is one of the sins that's mentioned that does grieve Him.

Let's look at one more aspect of lying. This one is a pet peeve of mine. I think "acting a lie" is just as bad as opening your mouth and telling one. I've seen this play out in the lives of devout Christians. This study has caused me to not overlook myself. So I've repented. I really can't recall an instance, but it's so easy to fall into.

I looked up the words *liar*, *lie*, and *lying*. *Lying* is the present participle of *lie*. According to *Merriam-Webster* dictionary, it means

"(1) to make an untrue statement with intent to deceive, (2) to create a false or misleading impression." The number 2 definition is the one that describes a person "acting a lie." Both definitions are acts of deception.

Let's be aware of our words, action, intentions, and motivations. In other words, let's guard our hearts, for out of it flows the issues of life (Proverbs 4:23).

Lastly, let's look at where deception comes from. It should turn our stomachs to think we're letting something as vile as Satan and his unclean spirits (demons) influence us to lie or give a false misleading impression (act a lie).

> And the great dragon was cast out, that old serpent, called the Devil, and Satan, which deceiveth the whole world: he was cast out into the earth, and his angels were cast out with him. (Revelation 12:9)

Day 43

Lady Lydia

Please read Acts 16:5–15.

God's Word is so rich in inspiring stories. I admonish you to read chapter 16 in its entirety. It's especially inspiring to see the Holy Spirit at work in the lives of those whom He uses to spread the Gospel message.

I cannot adequately tell you about Lady Lydia without talking about Paul and part of his missionary journey. It amazes me how God, through the working of the Holy Spirit, can cause lives to come together for the greater good, who are hundreds of miles apart and may not be aware of the existence of one another. When you have a hunger and thirst for God, He will move heaven and earth to satisfy that hunger.

> Blessed are they which do hunger and thirst after righteousness: for they shall be filled. (Matthew 5:6)

The Word says that Lydia, a business woman, a Gentile, worshipped God. How likely is it for a well-to-do business woman to worship and seek after the God of Israel, living in a Metropolitan city? How did she come to know about Israel's God? The Gospel had not been spread that far yet, but she knew enough to gather in hiding down by the river and pray on the Sabbath.

So here comes God reaching beyond many countries, forbidding Paul to go in a different way in order to get him to travel to this particular city in Philippi. God is so gracious. He gave Paul a dream of a man (someone) crying out in Macedonia. Could it have been this woman's prayers? What a mighty God we serve! A loving and kind God. He sees this woman crying out for help.

No doubt she didn't know the kind of help she or they needed, but God knew.

How wonderfully amazing it is to be led by the Holy Spirit. He still does that today for His children in Christ. If you're His, stay in prayer and especially in His Word with an open heart and listening ears, then you will perceive His leading and guiding you.

> My child, pay attention to what I say. Listen carefully to my words. Don't lose sight of them. Let them penetrate deep into your heart. (Proverbs 4:20–21 NLT)

> Trust in the LORD with all your heart; do not depend on your own understanding. Seek his will in all you do, and he will show you which path to take. (Proverbs 3:5–6 NLT)

God opened Lydia's heart so she could receive the good news about Jesus and receive salvation. There are people coming and sitting in worship services whose hearts are not opened to the Gospel message. I believe if you cry out to God in faith for someone you know and love, for God to open their heart, eventually you'll see the fruit of your labor. You may ask, "What if they don't go to church"? Isaiah 59:1 (NLT) says, "Listen! The LORD's arm is not too weak to save you, nor is his ear too deaf to hear you call."

My last two years of college at a major university, I did not go to church except one time. I started going after I moved and got a job, but my mind was not on Jesus at all. I was doing the socially acceptable thing to do. But God reached out and arrested me. I know it was my parents' prayers. Don't give up and stop praying for a loved one. I continue to thank God, for someone was praying for me.

Day 44

Lady Mary Magdalene

Read Matthew 27:56, 61 and 28:1; Mark 15:40, 47 and 16:1, 9; Luke 8:2 and 24:10; and John 19:25 and 20:1, 11, 16, 18.

Mary Magdalene is mentioned in all the Gospels in the New Testament. However, there is little known about her. We know that Jesus cast seven demons or unclean spirits out of her. And we know that she, after being set free from being possessed (controlled) by demonic spirits, became a follower of Christ. That's not much that we know, but that's a lot.

Let's examine these two facts that the Bible shares. Being possessed by an evil spirit cannot be good. Being possessed by seven evil spirits must make life a living hell. The *Merriam-Webster* dictionary defines *possessed* as "influenced or controlled by something (such as an evil spirit, a passion, or an idea." So we can surmise that she was not in control of what she did or how she acted. She may have been in pain, may have tried to harm herself or others. Examples of others in the Bible are found in

And when they were come to the multitude, there came to him a certain man, kneeling down to him, and saying, Lord, have mercy on my son: for he is lunatic, and sore vexed: for ofttimes he falleth into the fire, and oft into the water. Then Jesus rebuked the demon in the boy, and it left him. From that moment the boy was well. (Matthew 17:14–15, 18)

> And it came to pass, as we went to prayer, a certain damsel possessed with a spirit of divination met us, which brought her masters much gain by soothsaying: The same followed Paul and us, and cried, saying, These men are the servants of the most high God, which show unto us the way of salvation. And this did she many days. But Paul, being grieved, turned and said to the spirit, I command thee in the name of Jesus Christ to come out of her. (Acts 16:16–18)

And he came out the same hour.

Let's look at her reaction to being delivered or set free.

> And it came to pass afterward, that he went throughout every city and village, preaching and showing the glad tidings of the kingdom of God: and the twelve were with him, And certain women, which had been healed of evil spirits and infirmities, Mary called Magdalene, out of whom went seven devils. (Luke 8:1–2)

She was delivered out of darkness into the light of Jesus Christ. What a difference that made for her life. She began following Him everywhere He went, listened to His teachings, watched Him as He healed and set others free, and ministered to Him and His ministry.

> Joanna, the wife of Chuza, Herod's business manager; Susanna; and many others who were contributing from their own resources to support Jesus and his disciples. (Luke 8:3 NLT)

You see the love and devotion she exhibited as she followed Him right on to His crucifixion and being one of the first ones to witness His resurrection. She was probably among the 120 believers who were together on the Day of Pentecost. Read Acts 1.

What does this story about Mary Magdalene say to you? Should it be an example of our conversion today? Absolutely! When you get saved, in essence, you've been delivered out of darkness, out of the kingdom of Satan, into the kingdom of God's dear Son.

> Who hath delivered us from the power of darkness, and hath translated us into the kingdom of his dear Son. (Colossians 1:13)

You may not have been possessed, but you were influenced by Satan. We all were caught in his trap. So when you were set free, did you let everything else go and began to follow Jesus?

Were you drawn to His Word and began learning of Him, serving Him? Did you make a U-turn in life?

We should be like Mary Magdalene. Things of this world no longer satisfy us; but we should have a strong desire, hunger, or craving for the things of God. If that does not describe you, repent. Ask for God's forgiveness and for Him to give you that desire, that hunger, that thirst for Him. It all comes from Him. You must want it.

Think about what it took for salvation to be made available for you and me. Think about the sacrifice, the suffering He endured just for you and me. Think about what life would be like if we had continued on the road we were on. Think about what your afterlife would be like without Him. Thank You, Jesus, for salvation!

Day 45

Lady Lois and Lady Eunice

Read Acts 16:1, 3 and 2 Timothy 1:5, 3:15.

> I am reminded of your sincere faith, a faith that
> dwelt first in your grandmother Lois and your
> mother Eunice and now, I am sure, dwells in you
> as well. (2 Timothy 1:5 ESV)

If I were to give this blog a title other than the one above, I
would entitle it "Passing It On." Timothy's father was Greek and
probably not a believer. His mom was Jewish and a believer. The
Bible doesn't tell us about Timothy's grandfather. It doesn't appear
that the father nor the grandfather had a hand in teaching Timothy
the Scriptures and faith.

However, he had his grandmother, Lois, who taught her daughter, Eunice. Then the daughter, and maybe the grandmother, taught
him. Usually, you look to the father to be the spiritual leader in the
household. And that is wonderful if it happens. But what are you
going to do if the father doesn't take up that mantle or, as many times
in modern-day society, fathers are not present in the household? You
would think this is quite simple. The mom fulfills this role.

But I have witnessed Christian moms who say that's not her role
because the father is in the home. Excuse me! So you're going to let
your child(ren) grow up ignorant of God, His ways, and His Word
because your husband is not doing what he is supposed to be doing.

This is one thought I always had: *You only have one time around with your children, and you'd better start early. There are no do-overs.*

I'm not limiting what God can do in a child's life after he leaves your house. Furthermore, there are children who, because of their friends, neighbors or church bus ministries who reach out to provide a Christian education to them. One young lady told me she went to church and became a Christian because of her friends. God will use whoever is available and willing to get a soul saved.

However, that's not a chance I'm willing to take, that someone else will introduce my child to Jesus. When you give birth to a child, it's your responsibility to bring him or her to Jesus—not the preacher, Sunday school teacher, missionaries, neighbors, or anyone else.

Paul thought very highly of this disciple named Timothy. He traveled with Paul and Silas on some of his missionary journeys. He called him "my son in the ministry." He sent Timothy to be the leader of one of his church plants in Thessalonica and later in Ephesus.

Paul recognized that Timothy's unfeigned (sincere) faith came from his mother Eunice and grandmother Lois (2 Timothy 1:5). He also said this about Timothy in 2 Timothy 3:15, "And that from a child thou hast known the holy Scriptures, which are able to make thee wise unto salvation through faith which is in Christ Jesus."

These women started teaching him at an early age. And I assume through the synagogue also. He also observed their faith because the same faith in them was in him also.

My sincere desire is that young fathers and mothers would begin teaching their children about the ways of God at an early age. This is done through biblical instructions, faithful church attendance, and a lifestyle that exemplifies godliness and faith.

Day 46

Lady Johnnie Mae Johnson

This is my sister, best friend forever, confidant, and fellow woman of God who died on January 29, 2022. I wanted to share a glimpse of her life because she was a glorious example of Christlikeness. One of her grandsons wrote this tribute and shared it at her funeral. Maybe this will bless and encourage you.

I stayed up late last night reflecting on who my grandmother was during her time on this earth. I'm sure we will hear from others of her effectiveness as a minister, community leader, trailblazer, and friend.

All of these titles are wonderful; and as the obituary will reflect, she was a caring daughter, loving mother, attentive grandmother, beloved sibling, best friend, cherished aunt, in-law who would engraft those betrothed into the family with love.

Johnnie, Johnnie Mae, Mommy, Mama Johnnie, Aunt Johnnie, as my son cried out earlier this week the best GG in the world, and my personal favorite, Gran—all these nicknames pointed to the same person. Someone who *loved* her family. She cherished the word and work of her father Bubba Thompson so much she lived it out for us when she became the matriarch of the family.

She was in constant contact with her brothers and sister, keeping the bond strong. She really cared to know what was going on with immediate and extended family. She stressed the importance of communication and could communicate with you for hours if you let her. I'd give a lot for a few minutes now though. A communicator listens as well as talks. She was gifted with empathy, and it showed in her ability to take on what hurt you through her ears and build you up with her words that followed.

We all knew her as a praying woman, who recognized that her arms weren't very long but knew she could call the master whose reach was unlimited and mercy and grace never ran out. If you have Sheffield, Thompson, Montgomery, or Johnson blood, you can rest assured you've been prayed for by Johnnie Mae.

We knew she lived by faith. If you knew nothing else about her, you knew she loved God, recognized Jesus as Lord, lived with joy because He lives and desired for all those she came in contact with to share in His riches of mercy.

She celebrated her Lord and Savior in worship and praised Him with one of the most beautiful voices you'd ever hear.

She was full of joy and laughter. She had a wonderful laugh that was infectious enough to put a smile on your face no matter how you were feeling in the moment.

She was passionate. You could tell when something was very serious because her eyes would get big when she talked to you that you could almost see the fire in them and that let you know it's time to pay attention because this matters.

She was proud of her family. She loved the family reunions and seeing our tree grow. She loved to hear of our accomplishments, adventures, and achievements. She would bring them up to me when we talked about something that related. Sometimes I wouldn't know which family member she was talking about and she would ask, "You don't know your people? Mike, Mike, you need to know who your family is."

She was not a wealthy woman, but the wisdom she shared was worth a million times more than anything she could leave us in a will. Like when I was in college going through one of the lowest times of my life, I posted subliminal messages on Facebook because my pride succeeded in blocking me from asking directly for help. She called me out of the blue and said, "Boy, what's wrong with you?" I was a Coke, and her words were a Mentos drop that catalyzed an eruption, causing me to spill my guts in a pouring out of guilt and shame. After she let me finish, her voice changed, and she said, "Now you listen to me." She said, "Son, the number one trick of the enemy is guilt. If he can make you feel guilty, he can get you to take your eyes off of the rights you have as a child of God." That led me to Micah:

"Do not rejoice over me, my enemy! Though I have fallen, I will stand up; though I sit in darkness, the Lord will be my light. Because I have sinned against him, I must endure the Lord's rage until he champions my cause and establishes justice for me. He will bring me into the light; I will see his salvation" (Micah 7:8).

What she may have lacked in cash, she was rich in faith. When finances might have been few, she was abundant in dependency on Jesus. Where funds may have been low, her spirit was always high because she recognized the power of love, light, and the effect it would have on the world around her. And at the end of everything her resolve to fight on, do and say what's right no matter what stood in front of her as she would say was "it's okay because I'm going to be with Jesus."

For that, I am one of many of the most proud grandchildren in the world, and I pray to leave a similar legacy. (A tribute by Min. Michael Johnson Jr., her grandson)

Day 47

Lady Priscilla

Read Acts 18:2, 18, 26; Romans 16:3; 1 Corinthians 16:19; 2 Timothy 4:19; and Mark 10:7–8 (ESV).

> "Therefore a man shall leave his father and mother and hold fast to his wife, and the two shall become one flesh." So they are no longer two but one flesh. (Matthew 19:5)

Amazing! God set the pattern for marriage from the very beginning of time (Genesis 2:24). Jesus quotes it in Matthew and Mark. It was to be a permanent bond between man and woman. So as I examined the scriptural passages for information on Priscilla, I noticed an awesome phenomenon. Every time I see Priscilla's name, it's mentioned along with her husband's name, Aquila.

This couple's marriage personifies the scriptural passage cited above. Pricilla ministered, traveled, and worked alongside her husband. The Word said, "And they shall be one flesh." What does *one flesh* mean?

The website www.gotquestion.com sums it up so clearly to me:

> The biblical view of "one flesh" communicates a unity that covers every facet of a couple's joint lives as husband and wife. In marriage, two whole lives unite together as one emotionally, intellectually, financially, spiritually, and in every

other way. The "two shall become one" in purpose. They are so close that they function like one person, balancing each other's strengths and weaknesses so that together they can fulfill their God-given calling.

Being one flesh does not automatically happen once you are united in holy matrimony. Jesus said, "They shall become one flesh."

> But from the beginning of creation, "God made them male and female." "Therefore a man shall leave his father and mother and hold fast to his wife, and the two shall become one flesh." So they are no longer two but one flesh. (Mark 10:6–8)

Therefore, being one flesh is a process. But that also tells me that there must be a kingdom husband and a kingdom wife submitting to God's rules and God's ways. Both should be born-again believers; otherwise, you're headed for trouble.

> Be ye not unequally yoked together with unbelievers: for what fellowship hath righteousness with unrighteousness? and what communion hath light with darkness?
> And what concord hath Christ with Belial? or what part hath he that believeth with an infidel? (2 Corinthians 6:14–15)

That's where it should all start—from the beginning. Where are you going to find a believer, someone whose beliefs starts and ends with Jesus? Well, you probably will not find him or her in a bar or nightclub. It's not guaranteed you'll always find him or her at church. So what's the key?

Commit yourself to Jesus. Seek His will and His way.

Take the situation to Jesus. Follow His leading and guiding. Do things his way. Wait on Him. Remember, part of the definition of "one flesh" is two whole male and female uniting together. Work on being that whole person in Christ.

Starting marriage with a believer is only a starting point. Now the process begins as Jesus says, "They shall become one." Looking again at the above definition, "two whole lives unite together as one emotionally, intellectually, financially, spiritually, and in every other way. The 'two shall become one' in purpose."

It seems Priscilla and Aquila's marriage fits this mold. I can easily see Ephesians 5:21–31 operating in this couple's marriage. Oneness comes in a marriage that follows this recipe. They worked together (Acts 18:2–3). They traveled together (Acts 18:18). They ministered together (Acts 18:24–26). They held church in their home (1 Corinthians 16:19).

> Give my greetings to Priscilla and Aquila, my co-workers in the ministry of Christ Jesus. In fact, they once risked their lives for me. I am thankful to them, and so are all the Gentile churches. (Romans 16:3–4 NLT)

Day 48

Lady Tabitha, aka Dorcas

Read Acts 9:36–42.

> Now there was at Joppa a certain disciple named
> Tabitha, which by interpretation is called Dorcas:
> this woman was full of good works and alms
> deeds which she did. (Acts 9:36)

I pray that you'll read the whole story of Tabitha, but what caught my eye at this time was in verse 36. That first verse tells us that Tabitha was full of good works and did alms deeds. A great thing happened to her, but I'm led to discuss the great things she did.

This is why it caught my eye.

The Lord Jesus commanded us to "let your light so shine before men, that they may see your good works, and glorify your Father which is in heaven" (Matthew 5:16). In the fourteenth verse, He says we are the light of the world. What does a light do? It shines out into the darkness. The world is a dark and wicked place. God has given us the responsibility to reflect the light of Jesus. You know He said He is the light of the world (John 8:2). What did He do with His light? "He went about doing good and healing all that were sick" (Acts 10:38). Now He has gone to sit at the Father's right hand. But He left His light here in us. We're to reflect His light somewhat like the moon reflects the light of the sun.

How do we go about reflecting that light? The same way He did it—going about doing good works. He didn't say if you go to church, unbelievers would glorify His Father. He didn't say if you dress the part and look all pious that men would glorify His Father. He didn't say if you tell sinners they are sinning, they would glorify His Father.

No, he simply said when they see your good works, they would glorify His Father.

There is a saying that goes, "You can catch more bees with honey than with vinegar."

I look at the church. We hold a lot of assemblies throughout the week. Unbelievers see that. But does it draw them to glorify God? No, they just figure you're religious. Don't get it twisted though. We should and must, in obedience, assemble ourselves together. But that's where we stop. Where are our good deeds? Can anyone look at you and say you're full of good works? Or at your funeral, will they honestly say you were full of good works? Think about it.

Another thing we should consider is what Paul said in Ephesians 2:10: "For we are his workmanship, created in Christ Jesus unto good works, which God hath before ordained that we should walk in them."

You weren't saved because of your good works. But if you are saved, you are recreated in Christ to do good works. He is working in you and through you to effect positive change for others through your good works.

Why does good works work to draw others to glorify God? We hear it said or sung. "What the world needs now is love sweet love." They should see the love of Jesus Christ shining through your good works.

What are some good works? Mainly showing kindness to someone in need. Tabitha was kind to widows and the poor. She made coats and other clothing for widows and others. What skills do you have that you can use to help others? The world use the terms "acts of kindness" and "paying it forward." Make it your goal to do something kind for others on a regular basis. It could be a bill of groceries for someone, a phone call to a widow or ailing friend. It could be helping a mom pay the registration fee for her young athlete to participate in a sporting event. There is a number of things you can do. People see love through what you're giving or doing.

I will end this with other scriptures declaring the importance of good works.

Discover creative ways to encourage others and to motivate them toward acts of compassion, doing beautiful works as expressions of love. (Hebrews 10:24 TPT)

True Wisdom Comes from God If you are wise and understand God's ways, prove it by living an honorable life, doing good works with the humility that comes from wisdom. (James 3:13 NLT)

Having your conversation honest among the Gentiles: that, whereas they speak against you as evildoers, they may by your good works, which they shall behold, glorify God in the day of visitation. (1 Peter 2:12 KJV)

Day 49

Lady Phoebe

Read Romans 16:1–2.

Many women are mentioned only once in the Bible. But a lot can be deduced from what is said about the woman.

Paul holds Phoebe in high esteem as he introduces her to the Roman Church. This reminds me of when a Christian moves to another town and they move their church membership. When they decide which church they will attend, many times they will take a letter of recommendation from their previous pastor. I don't see that practiced much today. I never heard it taught, so I wondered why some do it and others don't. I didn't do it because I didn't know at the time it was a common practice nor why it was necessary to do. But I can see from this passage they may have been inspired to follow this example. There are several traditions or practices I've observed in the church that no one took the time to teach it or explain why it's done. I won't share them here because that's not what this article is about. But maybe you want to do some research on things you've observed in the Black church. Or maybe that will be another book for me to write.

Paul described her as a servant, Greek word *diakonos*, which means "minister, servant, or deacon or deaconess." The Bible dictionary further explains it to mean a leader, ruler. It sounds like she was a leader in the church. Paul encouraged them to assist her in whatever business she had. He also said she succored (KJV) to others and to him. *Succored* means "to help, aid, to furnish relief and aid those in danger."

This woman was definitely not a benchwarmer or spectator in church. She sounds like a true willing worker. Many times, especially denominational churches like the ones I grew up in and still a member of one, we identify a church worker as one who works in auxiliaries of the church.

We can really busy ourselves in these activities. And I must admit, some of them are necessary. If you don't join these auxiliaries, then you are looked upon as a benchwarmer.

But guess what! That's not the real work Jesus called us to. The real work is outside the walls of the church. If your church has some outreach ministry, that's where the real work is. If not, then you look around your neighborhood and find a place you can offer some relief. I used to complain about our lack of outreach ministries. Then I teamed up with some of our ladies, and we started providing help where needed. There is always something you can do to help others. Ask the Lord to show you where you can best serve. The Holy Spirit has some very creative ideas.

I have not researched this, but the early churches were held in someone's home. I don't know when they started erecting buildings. For fear of persecution, they had to keep their meeting places a secret. So there were no auxiliaries to "work" in.

Day 50

Read Romans chapter 16—Lady Mary (v. 6); Lady Andronicus and Lady Junia (v. 7); Lady Tryphena, Lady Tryphosa, and Lady Persis (v. 12); and Lady Julia and Lady Olympas (v. 15). Read Romans 16: 6, 7, 12, 15.

I have read Romans chapter 16 many times but never really paid much attention to these names. The only ones that I recognized or knew were Aquila and Priscilla, a husband-and-wife ministry team. The name Mary is a woman's name. There were one or two others that I recognized to be female names. I figured all the others were male names until doing this study. I'm not completely sure I got it right because some of the commentaries disagreed.

Some of Paul's writings and some teachings I've received led me to think women did not play a major role in the early church. Women were to learn in silence most of the time, not having a leadership role in the early church. There were pockets of women in leadership like Priscilla, Dorcas, and a few others. Although I knew within myself that women played a major role in the kingdom, especially when you looked in the Old Testament too, I have never done an in-depth study of the idea.

Can you imagine my surprise when I stumbled upon all these women whom Paul says were his fellow workers in spreading the Gospel. He gives several women accolades because they worked so hard in the church. These women were very busy, not sitting around being silent.

I noticed that the early churches were house churches. I assume it's because of all the persecutions that were going on. They didn't have large nor small building as we see today. Being Westerners, when we here of Paul establishing churches on his missionary journeys, we automatically think of a church building. We sometimes forget that we believers are the church.

In my search, I found out that the emperor of Rome, Constantine the Great, legalized Christianity in AD 313 after he became a Christian himself. They say it was a political move. Maybe so. But they began building church buildings after that. It didn't turn out to be all good because Constantine took authority over the Christian movement. But that's beside the point. That's another story for another time.

Many times Paul would greet the church that was in a person's house. But most of the church work was carried on outside the gathering. I've found that women preached and taught inside and outside the church gathering place. There were women who held church in their home.

The point I really want to make is that we women have a responsibility to work in the kingdom of God. We are not to be spectators but willing workers. We are called to a greater work than just busy "church work." We are called to help build the kingdom of God. Jesus told us in Matthew that more laborers were needed.

> Then saith he unto his disciples, The harvest
> truly is plenteous, but the laborers are few;
> Pray ye therefore the Lord of the harvest,
> that he will send forth laborers into his harvest.
> (Matthew 9:37–38)

Day 51

Lady Euodias and Lady Syntyche

Read Philippians 4:1–8.

Pronunciation of Euodias is *yoo-oh-dee-uhs*, and Syntyche is *sin-ti-kee.*

This is one thing I appreciate about God. He's authentic, keeps it real, or you might say He's transparent about what is reported in the Bible. He doesn't try to hide the imperfections of His people throughout the whole Bible. We, on the other hand, try to cover up imperfections in ourselves and others. "Don't give your testimony; it'll just be a gossip report." Not concerned that somebody might be helped by what someone else has gone through. We know better, but we want people to look perfect. It's like Jesus said, "There is none good, but one, that is God" (Matthew 19:17).

I thank God. He recognizes that even born-again names written in the Lamb's book of life believers will miss the mark sometimes. He's not shocked that even though we have His Holy Spirit living in us, we miss it sometimes. That's why we have repentance and the blood of Jesus. Jesus died not only for our past sins but our present and future sins as well.

As we look at Philippians 4:1–8, we see Paul expressing concern for two women who had a disagreement. Euodias and Syntyche were fellow workers with Paul in spreading the Gospel. He encourages them to agree and work in harmony in the Lord (Philippians 4:2 AMP). Then he proceeds to tell them, others, and ourselves how to be of the same mind, working in harmony with one another.

This is awesome. I've memorized verses 4 to 8 in the KJV translations throughout the years in an effort to maintain my peace, protect, and guard my heart and my thought life. I never took the time to tie in the first three verses not realizing they are the reason for the following verses.

If each and every individual in the body of Christ would practice this, there would not be any disagreements, only peace and harmony in the body of Christ. Each of us is only responsible for ourselves.

I will be using The Passion Translation (TPT) as I discuss this. The first thing Paul tells us to do is in every season of life, practice being cheerful and celebrating joyfully.

He says let your joy overflow. And you can do this because you're united with Christ. We're not depending on ourselves but on the one we're united with, Christ. All our strength and power come from him. We must let go and yield to Him. Meditating on these verses will help us accomplish all they are saying.

Next, he tells us to be gentle in how we relate to others. That can be another tall order. Since he tells us to rejoice in all seasons of life, he's saying be gentle in how you relate to others regardless of whether the relationship is favorable or unfavorable.

Verse 6 tells us instead of worrying, be saturated in prayer throughout the day. Talk to God about everything, every detail of your life. But make sure you're requesting in faith.

Then as verse 7 assures us as we do this, the peace that can only come from God and is pass human understanding will make the answer known to us through Christ Jesus. This is a reality to me. When I spend time rejoicing in praise and worship, I hear answers to problems, situations, and directions before I ask. Sometimes when I begin my day this way, I receive my "to-do list" for the day—things that I might forget to do. So I take time to write down what I hear. Awesome, awesome!

In verse 8, we're told to guard our hearts and minds. He tells us what to think on. He has already warned us in 2 Corinthians 10:4–5 that we have spiritual weapons to use to cast down though that are contrary to God's Word. Then we replace them with thoughts that are fixed on things that are true, honest, just, pure, lovely, and of good report.

I believe we've just received the prescription for walking in harmony with our fellow brothers and sisters in the Lord.

Day 52

Lady Mary, Mother of John Mark

Read Acts 12:11–17 and Colossians 4:10.

We first read of Mary in connection with Peter's miraculous release from prison by the angel of God. Read Acts 12:1–11. In verse 5, you will find that while Peter was kept in prison, "prayer was made without ceasing by the church."

Guess where the church was located—in the house of Mary, mother of John Mark. What does this tell you about Mary? The first thing I thought of was that she was very brave. The reason I say that is because you will find out how much persecution of the followers of Jesus was going on at the beginning of the chapter and that it pleased the Jews.

Herod had James, John's brother, killed. Then he proceeded to have Peter arrested but had to delay killing him because of the Days of Unleavened Bread. That story is so awe-inspiring, reading about what took place that night. First, I was amazed that Peter could sleep soundly while held by four bands of armed soldiers and in shackles. The angel had to shake him and raise him up. I long for sleep like that!

Mary knew that if she were caught holding church in her house, she and all who were with her could be imprisoned or killed. She was a devout woman of faith and believed in prayer.

She must have been a woman who was well-endowed to have a house big enough to hold church. It's also evident that she had servants. One was named Rhoda.

Furthermore, it appears that Mary was brought up in a God-fearing home and, in the course of time, became a believer. Her brother, Barnabas, was also a believer and traveled on many missionary journeys with Paul, who also took her son, John Mark, with him.

Mary was an example of courage and of faith to her son, John Mark, who later traveled with his uncle Barnabas and Paul on their missionary journeys. This young man is also the writer of the second book of the Gospels that bears his name: Mark.

The Bible doesn't tell us if she had a husband or was a widow. But I would imagine she held to the declaration that Joshua made: "As for me and my house we will serve the Lord" (Joshua 24:15). Moms, parents, if you want your children to grow up loving and living for the Lord, it's imperative that they see you loving and living for the Lord. If your children grow up seeing you go to church and you take them to church but when you get home, they don't see godly traits in you and God is not honored at home, they'll not likely love or live for the Lord. All they saw at home were religious practices.

Another scenario is if you use a dogmatic or dictatorial style of teaching your children. It's almost guaranteed to run them away from the Lord. Instead, lead by example and lovingly instruct them in the ways of the Lord. Don't forget to pray for them continuously.

Acknowledgements

I share a group text with my grandchildren and one great granddaughter who are mature enough to participate. They inspired the naming of this book. From oldest to youngest are Jeremy, Cassie, Andrew, Corey, Kayli, Kyle, Courtnee, Kameron and Ari.

I challenged them to suggest a name for this book. I had some awesome responses. I thank God for them and all my grands and great-grands.

I also thank God for my Husband Clent Holmes. He's strong, loves and supports me as I face many life challenges. My three living children and spouses; Terrell, Camille and Nick, Clent II and Sonya. They help me with my technological inefficiencies, advice and love. I also am appreciative for my stepsons whom I love, Clifton and Brendon.

About the Author

Helen Holmes is a retired school personnel who worked as a speech and language pathologist and head start director. She accepted her call into ministry in 1995. She founded a single moms ministry called SMILE (Single Moms Inspired to Live with Excellence). She taught both youth and adults in her local church. She founded a blog entitled *Women Seeking Intimacy with God*. This book is based on some of the blogs she wrote. In 2019, she cofounded a grief support group for moms who had experienced one or more child(ren) transition this life to the next. After her son, Greg, transitioned to heaven in October 2018, she partnered with a Christian sister whose daughter also transitioned to heaven in May 2018. They started this group in response to 1 Thessalonians 5:11, "Wherefore comfort yourselves together, and edify one another, even as also ye do."

www.ingramcontent.com/pod-product-compliance
Lightning Source LLC
Chambersburg PA
CBHW021001180726
47993CB00017B/500